BREAKING THE MOULD?

BREAKING THE MOULD?

The Birth and Prospects
of the Social Democratic Party

IAN BRADLEY

Martin Robertson · Oxford

First published in 1981
by Martin Robertson & Company Ltd., 108 Cowley Road,
Oxford OX4 1JF.
Reprinted October 1981

British Library Cataloguing in Publication Data

Bradley, Ian, *1950–*
    Breaking the mould?
    1.   Social Democratic Party – History
    I.   Title
    324.2410972   JN1129.S/

    ISBN 0-85520-468-0
    ISBN 0-85520-469-9 Pbk

Typeset by Oxford Verbatim Limited
Printed and bound in Great Britain by Book Plan Limited, Worcester

For Lucy

Contents

Acknowledgements

The original idea for this book came in a telephone call from Jo Grimond. For him the birth of the Social Democratic Party is an event which arouses conflicting emotions. It may well bring about the realignment of British politics which he has long hoped to see and for which he worked as leader of the Liberal Party from 1956 to 1967. Yet at the same time he has a lurking fear that for all their rhetoric the leaders of the new party may simply be offering a rehash of the old corporatist state socialism which they practised while they were in the Labour Party. I share both these feelings. This book is written from a point of view which is at once both sympathetic and sceptical towards its subject.

As well as from two stimulating and highly enjoyable conversations with Jo Grimond, I have greatly benefited in the preparation of this book both from formal interviews and informal conversations with Roy Jenkins, David Owen, Shirley Williams, William Rodgers, David Marquand, Dick Taverne, Jim Daly, Douglas Eden, Alec McGivan, Roger Liddle, Matthew Oakeshott, Colin Phipps, Michael Barnes, Roger Morgan, Caroline Thomson, Richard Newby and Norman Hart. Where quoted remarks appear in the text which are not attributed to other sources, they were made in the course of these interviews and conversations.

John Lyttle and Mary Morgan in the SDP Press Office and Max Madden and his colleagues in the Labour Party Press Office have dealt with my enquiries cheerfully and efficiently. Robert Worcester and Brian Gosschalk of MORI have helped me greatly with poll data, and I am also grateful to Gallup and NOP for allowing me to quote from their polls.

The cartoons which are reproduced in this book are by

Martin of the *Sunday Express* (p. 9), Jak of the *New Standard* (p. 27), Calman of *The Times* (p. 43), Heath of the *Spectator* (p. 67), Garland of the *Daily* and *Sunday Telegraph* (pp. 72 and 87), Gibbard of the *Guardian* (p. 96), McAllister of the *Guardian* (pp. 105, 109 and 138) and Ford of the *Star* (p. 161). I am grateful to all of them for permission to reproduce their work.

I have had consistent support and encouragement from Michael Hay and Sue Corbett at Martin Robertson and from David Martin at Basil Blackwell Publisher. I would also like to thank my bosses at *The Times* for giving me a month's unpaid leave to write this book and for allocating to me the fascinating task of covering the birth of the SDP. I need only add that, of course, I alone am responsible for any mistakes which may occur in the following pages.

I.C.B.
26 July 1981

List of Abbreviations

The following abbreviations are used in this book:

ASL	Audience Selection Limited
CLV	Campaign for Labour Victory
EEC	European Economic Community
MORI	Market Opinion and Research International
NATO	North Atlantic Treaty Organisation
NEC	National Executive Committee of the Labour Party
NOP	National Opinion Poll
ORAC	Opinion Research and Communication
ORC	Opinion Research Centre
PLP	Parliamentary Labour Party
SDA	Social Democratic Alliance
SDP	Social Democratic Party
SPD	Sozialdemokratische Partei Deutschlands

Chronology: Steps Towards a Breakaway

1960   November   Campaign for Democratic Socialism
                        launched.

1971   28 October   Sixty-nine Labour MPs defy three-line
                        whip in vote of principle on entry into
                        the EEC.

1972   16–17 April   Roy Jenkins resigns deputy leadership
                        of the Labour Party, George Thomson
                        and Harold Lever resign from Shadow
                        Cabinet, Dick Taverne and David Owen
                        resign as front-bench spokesmen over
                        decision to hold referendum on con-
                        tinued membership of the EEC.

1973   1 March   Dick Taverne wins Lincoln by-election
                        as Democratic Labour candidate.
        October   Taverne launches Campaign for Social
                        Democracy

1974   17 December   Manifesto Group of Labour MPs
                        formed.

1975   March–June   EEC referendum campaign.
        17 June   Social Democratic Alliance (SDA)
                        formed.

1977   19 February   Campaign for Labour Victory (CLV)
                        launched.

1979	3 May	General Election. Shirley Williams loses her seat.
	July	David Marquand's article 'Inquest on a Movement' appears in *Encounter*.
	22 November	Roy Jenkins's Dimbleby Lecture.
	30 November	William Rodgers says in speech at Abertillery that the Labour Party has one year to save itself.
	20 December	Colin Phipps convenes meeting of Jenkinsites.
1980	31 May	Labour Party special conference at Wembley endorses 'Peace, Jobs, Freedom'.
	7 June	David Owen, Shirley Williams and Bill Rodgers say they will leave Labour Party if it commits itself to withdrawal from EEC.
	9 June	Roy Jenkins's Press Gallery lecture.
	15 June	Labour Party Commission of Inquiry votes for electoral college and endorses mandatory re-selection of MPs.
	24 July	SDA says it will put up candidates against Labour left-wingers.
	1 August	'Gang of Three' write open letter to fellow members of the Labour Party.
	9 September	David Marquand speaks at Liberal Party Assembly. David Steel gives Labour rebels six months to leave party.
	22 September– 3 October	Labour Party conference at Blackpool. Shirley Williams and Tom Bradley refuse to speak from platform on behalf of NEC. Conference votes to change method of electing leader and in favour of unilateral disarmament and withdrawal from EEC.
	10 November	Michael Foot elected leader of Labour Party.

21 November	David Owen says he will not be seeking re-election to Shadow Cabinet.
28 November	Shirley Williams says she cannot stand as Labour candidate on present policies.
1 December	SDA proscribed by Labour Party.

1981		
	6 January	Roy Jenkins returns from Brussels.
	14 January	First meeting of 'Gang of Four' in Shirley Williams's flat.
	18 January	'Gang of Four' meets in William Rodgers's house to draw up joint statement.
	24 January	Labour Party special conference at Wembley votes to give trade unions major say in election of party leader.
	25 January	'Gang of Four' issues Limehouse Declaration and launches Council for Social Democracy.
	26 January	Nine Labour MPs join Council for Social Democracy.
	30 January	David Owen tells his constituency party he will not stand as Labour candidate in next election.
	5 February	'Declaration of a Hundred' supporting Council published in *Guardian*. CLV breaks up and Alec McGivan becomes full-time organiser of Council.
	9 February	Council moves into offices in Queen Anne's Gate. Shirley Williams resigns from Labour's national executive.
	17 March	Conservative MP Christopher Brocklebank-Fowler crosses floor of Commons to join Council for Social Democracy.
	26 March	Launch of Social Democratic Party in Connaught Rooms.

CHAPTER 1

Introduction

The road to the Connaught Rooms

Nine o'clock in the morning is an unacceptably early hour for most journalists to start work – doubly so for those in the lobby who are used to a working day which begins when the House of Commons starts its business early in the afternoon and frequently does not end until nearly midnight.

Yet there was no shortage of political journalists reporting for duty at that hour at the Connaught Rooms, an elegant banqueting suite in the West End of London, on Thursday, 26 March 1981. They included two of the best-known faces on British television, Sir Robin Day and Professor Robert Mackenzie, and just about every political editor, correspondent, sketch writer and columnist in Fleet Street.

Nor was it only British journalists who were there. The major American and European television networks had more than two dozen camera crews in position at the back of the richly decorated baroque-style Grand Hall. Many of them had last been in London to record the Iranian Embassy siege in May 1980. The London correspondents of most of the world's major newspapers and press agencies swelled the throng of more than 500 inside the hall.

What had drawn them all to this unlikely venue was the launching of a new political party. That in itself was not an event rare enough to account for the crowds who assembled on the morning of 26 March. Only six months before I had attended a press conference, held at the rather more civilised hour of half-past three, in the upper room of an Italian restaurant in Chancery Lane to launch the New Britain Party, an amalgamation of the United Country Party and the Keep Britain United Party. Yet despite the presence of Mr Patrick Moore, the astronomer and television personality, who confidently stated that the new party was 'neither left-wing, nor right-wing, but stands for common sense', that launching attracted only a handful of journalists and received only minimal coverage in the following day's papers.

The party which was being launched in the Connaught Rooms, on the other hand, was a much more serious proposition. Its founders, the 'Gang of Four' (as they had generally become known over the previous few months), had all held senior ministerial posts in Labour Governments. They were Mr Roy Jenkins, a former Chancellor of the Exchequer and Home Secretary, who had just returned from a four-year spell as President of the European Commission in Brussels; Dr David Owen, a former Foreign Secretary; Mr William Rodgers, a former Minister of Transport; and Mrs Shirley Williams, a former Secretary of State for Education and one of the most popular and widely loved figures in post-war British politics. Before it had even been launched or faced an election, the party already had fourteen MPs and the support, according to opinion polls, of about 30 per cent of the electorate.

Perhaps what attracted journalists most about the launching of this particular party was the chance that it seemed to offer of breaking the firm mould in which British politics has been set for most of the twentieth century. Its name, the Social Democratic Party, struck a curious note in British ears. The only body of any consequence to have had a similar title before was the Marxist-orientated Social Democratic Federation, which had been active in the early days of socialism at the end of the nineteenth century. More recently, however, the term 'social democrat' had been used by those right-wing or 'moderate' members of the Labour Party who wished to distance themselves from the left wing of the party. In 1973 Dick Taverne, former Labour MP for Lincoln, had broken away from the party and launched his own Campaign for Social Democracy. Two years later a group of Labour councillors had formed the Social Democratic Alliance. Journalists had seized on these and other similar movements in the 1970s as signals of an impending split in the Labour Party and the emergence of a new radical centre party. Now at last it looked as though the event which they had been predicting for so long might actually be happening.

The scene in the Connaught Rooms had an atmosphere of show-business razzmatazz unusual in British politics. Girls in blazers festooned with red, white and blue SDP stickers handed out glossy press kits to the arriving journalists. The launch itself was conducted like a television quiz show, with the party's press officer, John Lyttle, acting as compere at a desk to the right of the room. In the centre, in front of enormous panels bearing the party's initials in the same style as the girls' badges, sat the stars of the show, the party's four founders. To the left were the supporting cast of MPs and members of the steering committee. The party had even brought along its own audience of distinguished supporters, including several peers of the realm, who sat in the gallery at the back of the Grand Hall and applauded enthusiastically at appropriate moments.

Mr Lyttle's first words to the expectant throng set the tone of the launch: 'I would be grateful if you could stand up when you ask questions so that the directional microphone can pick you up.' This was the party of the new age of high technology and instant electronic communication. Moments after the press conference started telephone banks were opened in twenty-one centres across the country to take calls from those who wanted to join. After they had paid their subscription directly by credit card, their names and addresses were fed into a computer, which had already sent out membership forms to more than 30,000 people who had expressed an interest in the new party in the three months before its launch.

On the strength of this computerisation of the new party's membership, the SDP leaders talked excitedly of introducing new forms of democratic participation into British politics, with members voting regularly on policy issues through postal referenda. They even suggested that there would be no need for them to follow the time-honoured ritual practised by the existing parties of holding annual conferences by the seaside every autumn. (In the event, they plumped for a three-stage conference, starting in Perth, continuing in Bradford and ending up in London.) At the same time they made it clear that they intended their message to be heard in every part of the country. Air taxis and high-speed trains were standing by to whip the 'Gang' off after the London launch to a series of smaller launches in regional centres. The City public relations firm which had planned the £175,000 launching campaign already had 'advance men' in these centres to smooth the way and was providing 'hand-holders' to accompany the 'Gang' throughout the day.

It was an appropriate start for a party which, in many ways, was the creation of the new class of journalists, marketing men, scientists and technologists who were in the van of Britain's transformation from an industrial to a post-industrial society. Half-way through the launch in the Connaught Rooms a journalist from the Soviet paper *Pravda* turned to me and asked, 'Would I be right if I told my readers that this marks the start of American-style politics in Britain?'

Perhaps European-style might be a better description. If the name of the new party sounded strange to British journalists, it had a distinctly familiar ring to those from the Continent. Its initials bore a remarkable similarity to those of the West German Sozialdemokratische Partei Deutschlands (SPD), arguably the most successful and the strongest political party in modern Europe. In its policies, its style and its outlook the new British party had modelled itself closely on the social democratic parties which were a familiar feature of the political landscape throughout most of the rest of northern Europe. In many ways, indeed, its foundation was a logical consequence of Britain's arrival in the EEC eight years earlier, a sign that we had become fully European.

Amid all the technological wizardry the launch was also being recorded in a more traditional medium. Perched precariously between the television cameras and lights at the back of the hall was a small artist's easel, at which John Bawtree, a Royal Academician who normally specialises in landscapes, was busy trying to capture the scene in oils. He had hurried back from a painting holiday in France when he heard the date of the launch, in the hope, as he put it, of 'catching a moment of history'.

There was certainly no doubt about the historic importance which the 'Gang of Four' themselves attached to the occasion. Mr Jenkins described it as 'the biggest break in English politics for two generations. We offer not only a new party but a new politics.' Mr Rodgers talked of it as 'an historic occasion' and Mrs Williams of 'a fresh beginning'.

Will 26 March 1981 in fact, go in the text books as a significant date in British political history? Is the Limehouse Declaration, issued by the 'Gang of Four' exactly two months before they launched their new party, destined to become as famous as Sir Robert Peel's Tamworth Manifesto or Joseph Chamberlain's Unauthorised Programme? Will the by-election campaign which Roy Jenkins fought in Warrington go into the same category as W. E. Gladstone's great Midlothian campaign? Or is the Social Democratic Party going to sink without trace, like the New Party launched by Sir Oswald Mosley in somewhat similar circumstances almost exactly fifty years earlier?

Inevitably, at this early stage in the party's life any assessment of its ultimate prospects and significance can be only very tentative. There are other questions, however, which can more easily be answered now. How did the Social Democratic Party come about? Why did its founders break away from the Labour Party? Who are the people involved in it, and where does its support come from? What are its policies? Later chapters will seek to present as clear and full an account as possible of the origins and birth of the SDP, the policies it stands for and the sort of people who are joining and supporting it.

New political parties have both very precise and quite intangible origins. Some schoolboys still learn that the Liberal Party was born at a meeting of Whigs, Radicals and Peelites in Willis's Assembly Rooms in St James's (a venue not unlike the Connaught rooms) on 6 June 1859. The birth of the Labour Party can be dated with similar precision to a conference in London on 27 February 1900 which inaugurated the Labour Representation Committee.

Yet few historians would attach too much significance to those particular dates or the events which took place on them. They are simply convenient signposts to developments which were in reality spread over a much longer timescale. The formation of the Liberal Party can be dated to as early as the late 1840s, with the arrival of Richard Cobden in Parliament, or as late as the late 1860s, with the election of Gladstone's first Liberal Government. The Labour Party could equally well be said to have begun in the early 1890's, when working-class candidates first stood against Liberals, or in 1906, when those elected first called themselves Labour Party MPs. Wider social and intellectual movements, which it is impossible to date precisely, also played their part in creating the climate in which the new parties grew. They included, for example, the transfer of wealth and influence from land to capital and the awakening of enlightened optimism in the case of the Liberals, and the rise of a collectivised proletariat and the development of the philosophy of socialism in the case of the Labour Party.

The same is true in the case of the SDP. It may well be that future historians will find its origins in Dick Taverne's by-election victory in Lincoln in 1973 or in the revolt of Labour pro-Marketeers against their party's basic opposition to Britain's membership of the EEC throughout the early 1970s. Some may even look as far back as the Campaign for Democratic Socialism of the early 1960s. At one level, the party is the creation of the 'Gang of Four' and their advisers, something which started as a gleam in the eye of Roy Jenkins as he contemplated his return to British politics from his desk in Brussels, and which became a reality when he joined forces with a handful of other disillusioned and dissatisfied Labour politicians. At a deeper level, however, it can be seen as a response to many of the most striking social and intellectual changes in Britain over the last few decades: the transition from an industrial to a service economy; the breakdown of traditional class loyalties; the rising protest against corporatism, centralisation and bureaucracy; the growing national mood of self-doubt and demoralisation.

Like all political parties, the SDP is as much the child of circumstance as it is the product of conscious creation or of the inevitable logic of history. Just as much responsible for its birth as the 'Gang of Four' who stole the show at the Connaught Rooms was another quartet of Labour politicians who took no pleasure at all in its arrival. If Sir Harold Wilson and James Callaghan had stood up more to the left when they were Labour leaders and proved more accommodating to the social democrat viewpoint, if Michael Foot had not then succeeded them as leader, and perhaps above all if Tony Benn had not embarked on his crusade first for a referendum on the EEC and then to democratise the party, the social democrats would never have broken away. This other 'Gang of Four' should at least get some of the credit for the new party's launch.

The story which this book tells contains many paradoxes. There is the curious fact that a social democratic party should be born just at the time when the British electorate seems to have signalled that it has lost its faith in social democracy. There is the clear dichotomy among its supporters between those who want it to be a brand-new, radical centre party of a kind never seen before in British politics and those who see it rather as a Mark II Labour Party which will stand for the old traditions of Gaitskellite social democracy. There is the fact that the party has most support in the traditionally Conservative rural and suburban areas of the South and least in the industrial Labour heartlands where most of its MPs have their constituencies. Perhaps above all there is the supreme paradox that if the SDP does well at the next election, it could well let in a left-wing Labour Government – the very thing that it was set up to prevent.

Very few people are neutral about the new party. For its supporters and members, many of whom have never had anything to do with a political party before, it has almost the status of a religious crusade. In their eagerness to hear the new gospel preached by their leaders and to bear witness to their faith, they have resurrected that almost defunct institution, the political meeting. When David Owen spoke at a school hall in Taunton, Somerset, on the evening of the March launch, more than a thousand people came to see and hear him. There had been no comparable gathering in the town since Winston Churchill had spoken there thirty years before. Almost equally large crowds have packed subsequent meetings held by the 'Gang of Four' throughout the length and breadth of Britain.

For its opponents, on the other hand, the SDP is almost entirely the creation of the media and the public relations men and offers a hollow set of trendy platitudes to the electorate. Michael Foot, who compared its policy statement with the 'infamous prospectus of the South Sea Bubble', told his constituency party that any company selling soap or soft drinks which asked subscribers to forward cash on the kind of pretence the SDP had adopted would soon be had up for fraud.[1] Critics point out that not one of the sitting MPs who have joined the new party has had the courage to take his case to the electorate by resigning and fighting a by-election. Some also wonder how far leopards can change their spots, reflecting that the Shirley Williams who now rails against trade unions and the power of their block vote is the same Shirley Williams who stood on the Grunwick picket line and who never complained about the block vote as long as it was supporting the right in the Labour Party. Others take a more detached and philosophical view, like Mr Harold Grose, a retired union shop steward and longtime Labour Party member in David Owen's Plymouth, Devonport, constituency:

Folks will soon forget they ever happened. In five years they'll be finished. The left and right of the Labour Party go in and out like the tides. The left happen to be in at the moment but it will all change and the Social Democrats will be left stranded just as Ramsay Macdonald, and Philip Snowden and all the others who have left the party have been.[2]

These conflicting views of the SDP are crystallised in contradictory assessments of the characters of its founders, both of which have wide currency. Seen from one point of view, the 'Gang of Four' are among the most honest, courageous and talented of modern British politicians. Roy Jenkins is seen as the most successful post-war Chancellor of the Exchequer and as a statesman of European dimension, Shirley Williams as sincere and approachable, David Owen as a tough and attractive young radical, Bill Rodgers as the epitome of all that is best in the Labour social democratic tradition. Seen from the opposite point of view, they are all essentially failed politicians who have set up the SDP as a salvage vessel for their tattered careers. From this perspective, Roy Jenkins emerges as a somewhat lazy *bon viveur* casting around for something which will blot out the memory of his failures as President of the EEC, Shirley Williams as 'a somewhat indecisive woman, of middling intellectual attainments and mistaken views'[3] who lost her seat in the 1979 election on a bigger swing than the national average, David Owen as a man who was over-promoted at too young an age and whose career was effectively at an end after his disappointing showing as Foreign Secretary, and William Rodgers as nothing more nor less than a former Minister of Transport.

The truth, as always, lies somewhere in between. No doubt the 'Gang of Four' would not have moved out of the Labour Party if their own prospects inside it had been better. But in breaking away to form a brand-new party they were taking an immense risk which one can only admire. The road which had brought them and their supporters to the Connaught Rooms on that March day was a bumpy one, which had involved many hard choices and much searching of consciences. It was a

Roll up, roll up, roll up! Try our marvellous cure-all! Brought to you by the people who made the Labour Party what it is today!
(Sunday Express, 2 January 1981)

long, winding trail that had taken them through many places together. For some it had started in Scarborough in 1960, for others at Königswinter on the banks of the Rhine in the early 1970s, for several on pro-EEC platforms around the country during the 1975 referendum campaign. For all of them, more recently, Brighton, Blackpool and Wembley had been important stages en route. Although there were many twists and turns along the way, there was a certain inevitability about the direction in which the road had always pointed: towards a final break with Labour and the establishment of a new social democratic party. The following chapters will chart that road and will aim to find out where it will eventually lead from the Connaught Rooms.

CHAPTER 2

The British Political Tradition

Adversarial politics and the quest for the centre ground

Any group breaking away from one of the established political parties in Britain starts with the odds heavily stacked against it. That is the lesson of history. In the last 150 years there have been around a dozen such breakaway movements. Only two of them have survived to become major political parties. The rest lasted for only a few years before withering away or rejoining one of the main parties.

The British political system has traditionally been one of the most stable and straightforward in the world. At its heart has been the two-party system, with first Whigs and Tories, then Liberals and Conservatives and finally Labour and Conservatives alternating in government. Such a simple choice has generally satisfied the electorate and has represented, accurately enough, the main divisions of opinion within the country. The central point of W. S. Gilbert's famous observation about every boy and girl being born either a little Liberal or else a little Conservative has held good since he put the words into the mouth of Private Willis, on sentry duty outside the Houses of Parliament, in *Iolanthe* in 1882.

There have, it is true, been periods when sizeable third parties have sat in the House of Commons and when politics has been dominated by splits and coalitions. This happened most notably between 1914 and 1935. Ultimately, however, the two-party system has always triumphed. The graves of failed breakaway parties, from the Liberal Unionists in the 1880s to the Common Wealth Party in the 1940s, stand out from the political history of modern Britain as silent warnings to those who would contemplate a similar move in the 1980s.

The political scene, however, has not been static. Two new parties have been born since the Great Reform Bill of 1832 established the modern style of British politics. Roughly sixty years separated their births. Another sixty years has now passed since Labour replaced the Liberals as the main force on the left in British politics. Has the time come for another change? Before answering that question it is worth taking a closer look at the political history of the last 150 years, and particularly at the British party system.

The one constant element throughout the period has been a strong and united Conservative Party. With its remarkable capacity for organic change and its solid appeal to the self-interest of the propertied and aspiring classes and to the deference of a section of the working classes, added to its unique ability to inspire loyalty and unity within its own ranks, it has managed to weather every political storm and to govern for longer than any other party.

The Conservatives have had to face remarkably few splits and breakaway groups since Disraeli re-established them in the 1860s as a popular party capable of forming a government. Rebellion against the leadership and desertion from the party are seen as particularly ungentlemanly acts in Tory circles. When Christopher Brocklebank-Fowler, MP for Norfolk North-West, joined the Social Democrats on the opposition benches on 16 March 1981, he was the first Conservative MP to cross the floor of the House of Commons since Austin Taylor defected to the Liberals in 1906.

While the Conservatives have been the most permanent and united element in the party system, the two main parties which have opposed them in elections and in Parliament have had a more temporary and divided character. In contrast to the Tories, who, like the poor, have somehow always been around and whose origins go back deep into the seventeenth century, both the Liberal and Labour Parties have arrived on the political scene in the last 150 years. Formed initially as coalitions of widely divergent interests and groups, they both underwent a distinct process of development before coming to maturity. The Liberals then disintegrated and declined in the period from 1914 to 1926; perhaps the Labour Party is about to go the same way in the 1980s.

In a book which seeks to analyse the significance of the Social Democratic Party it is worth looking briefly at the births of the Liberal and Labour parties. By doing so we can perhaps establish some of the factors which make for a seismic change, as distinct from a mere hiccup, in British politics. We can also begin to answer the question of whether the SDP is destined to join that small and select company of new parties which have succeeded in establishing themselves as the main alternatives to the Conservatives, or whether it will go down in history along with such ill-fated and half-remembered ventures as the New Party launched by Sir Oswald Mosley and other defectors from the Labour Party exactly fifty years earlier.

At one level the Liberal Party was created in the 1850s and 1860s as a result of a breakaway movement in some ways very similar to that which produced the SDP. Its Parliamentary leaders, William Ewart Gladstone, Edward Cardwell, the Duke of Argyll and others, had all been members of the Conservative Party in the 1840s. They were close followers and admirers of Sir Robert Peel, the Tory Prime Minister from 1841 to 1846.

It is not altogether fanciful to compare Peel with Hugh Gaitskell. Both men had remarkably similar personalities, with formidable intellectual capabilities that produced a slightly cold and diffident manner. More importantly, they shared a political aim – to make their respective parties credible instruments of government capable of carrying out substantial but sensible reforms to the social and economic structure of the nation. Both had to battle against ideological forces in their parties, Peel against protectionism and Gaitskell against unilateralism and the movement for more nationalisation. Early death robbed both of them of the chance to establish political structures which gave lasting embodiment to their political principles. Peel was unable to construct a new party dedicated to the policies of free trade, sound government and administrative reform after he had split the Tories over his repeal of the Corn Laws in 1846. Gaitskell, although victorious in his battle with the left over unilateral disarmament, failed in his other battle to expunge Clause Four from the Labour party constitution and to commit the party firmly to European-style social democracy.

After their leader's death in 1850, the Peelites remained a cohesive group in Parliament, distinctly separate from the protectionist bulk of the Tory Party led by the Earl of Derby and Benjamin Disraeli. During the 1850s they found themselves increasingly in sympathy with many Whig and Radical MPs. The meeting between these three groups which took place in Willis's Assembly Rooms in St James's, London, on 6 June 1859, when they agreed to combine to bring down Derby's Government, is generally taken to mark the birth of the Liberal Party.

This realignment at Westminster was, however, only one factor in the formation of the Liberal Party, and almost certainly not even the most important one. Gladstone and his colleagues in Parliament were able to form a new party principally because they could appeal to a new constituency in the country. In part it was literally a new constituency, created by the Reform Acts of 1832 and 1867, which enfranchised the middle classes and skilled working classes. In part it was the result of deep social, economic and intellectual changes and of widespread dissatisfaction with the existing political parties.

The Liberal Party was the child of the Industrial Revolution in Britain. Its birth was the inevitable consequence of the movement of economic power and social influence from landowners to manufacturers and merchants. It represented the coming of age of the middle classes. More generally, the formation of the British Liberal Party was part of a liberal awakening which took place throughout Europe in the middle of the nineteenth century and which manifested itself in a new spirit of tolerance and anti-clericalism, a concern with civil rights and representative democracy, and a profound reverence for freedom and individual liberty.

In Britain the particular spur to the creation of a new party was given by the existence of a number of powerful groups in the community which felt themselves to be alienated and excluded from the prevailing political system. Industrialists and businessmen found that their interests were not represented by a Parliament still dominated by landed interests. Nonconformists were increasingly angry about the privileges enjoyed by the Established Church. Those in the up-and-coming professional middle classes found their careers frustrated by patronage and aristocratic place-hunters. The skilled working class was being newly educated and radicalised by cheap newspapers and the growth of provincial consciousness.

The Whigs were scarcely less attractive than the Tories to all these groups, which wanted a new style of politician of the type of Richard Cobden, a calico printer in Lancashire who had led the successful campaign against the Corn Laws. With their common sense of alienation from the existing political system, they came together to form the backbone of the Liberal Party.

The new party took some time to establish itself. Twenty-one years elapsed between Cobden's taking his seat in the House of Commons and Gladstone's formation of the first Liberal Government in 1868. It was to be even longer before the Whigs' dominance over the party in Parliament was eroded. The old party lingered on within the new one for a long time, and throughout its life the Liberal Party remained a coalition of disparate, and even sometimes contradictory, interests and forces.

With the establishment of the Liberal Party and the reconstruction of the Tory Party by Disraeli, British politics took on its familiar adversarial character. In Parliament MPs of the two parties sat ranged opposite each other while their leaders engaged in gladiatorial combat. In the country political allegiances mirrored existing divisions in society. Religion was an important determinant of party loyalty, with Anglicans generally supporting the Tories and Nonconformists the Liberals. Social class, geographical location and even occupation were also important; northeners, skilled working men and mill owners tended to favour the Liberals, and southerners, the upper middle classes and brewers favoured the Conservatives.

The formation and rise of the Labour Party at the beginning of the twentieth century came about as the result of a similar confluence of social economic and intellectual change, alienation from the existing system and quite independent happenings at Westminster. Without the development of a class-conscious trade union movement and the emergence of socialism to challenge liberalism as the main ideology of the left in Europe, the British Labour Party would never have been born. Without the help which it was given by Liberal politicians in its early days and the disastrous effect on the Liberal Party produced by the split between its two leading figures during and after the First World War, it would never have emerged as the main opposition party to the Tories.

Of all the factors that brought about the birth of the Labour Party, the emergence of class as the main determinant of political behaviour in Britain was undoubtedly the most important. As its name implies, Labour grew up first and foremost as a class party, the aim of which was to give political expression to the new-found collective consciousness of the working classes. Just as the Liberal Party had been a child of the first stage of the Industrial Revolution, born of the rise of the manufacturing and commercial bourgeoisie, so the Labour Party was the child of its second stage, the development of mass production and the spread of the factory system. It was born out of the rise of the proletariat, a class which, because of its working and living experience, thought primarily in collective rather than in individual terms.

Like the Liberals also, the Labour Party owed its formation partly to the emergence of a new body of voters in the country and partly to the development of a new ideology. It too benefited from the extension of the electorate as a result of the Reform Acts of 1884 and 1918, which enfranchised working men and women. It also appealed to a group which the Liberal Party had alienated, the growing number of working men who, under the influence of the burgeoning trade union movement and the spread of socialist ideas, were coming to see the Liberals as implacable class enemies. Once the Liberals appeared in the guise of capitalists and employers, as opposed to leaders and fellow campaigners for radical causes, their support among the working classes began to be at risk.

Just as those who formed the Liberal Party included an important group which had broken away from the Tories, so the founders of the Labour Party included a significant number of people who had started their political lives in the Liberal Party. Three men in particular, who were later to be leading Labour politicians, first tried to embark on political careers in the Liberal Party but found that because of their working-class origins and socialist views they were unacceptable as candidates. Keir Hardie unsuccessfully sought adoption at mid-Lanark in 1888, Ramsay MacDonald in Southampton in 1894 and Arthur Henderson at Newcastle-on-Tyne in 1895. It was their experience at the hands of Liberal constituency associations, more than any other single factor, that prompted them to stand as independent Labour candidates and to set about creating their own party.

As much as the Liberals, the Labour Party was from the beginning a coalition of different interests. Although working-class consciousness, as expressed by the trade union movement, and alienation from the Liberals because of their identification with the interests of employers provided the main motivation for supporters and voters in the country, the leadership was equally influenced by ideological considerations. Socialist ideas, first developed and propagated in Britain by middle-class intellectuals in the Social Democratic Federation and the Fabian Society, contributed to the formation of the Labour Party, along with the more pragmatic and less theoretical demands of the trade unions. Those two elements, often incompatible and sometimes downright contradictory, have continued to coexist, peacefully and not so peacefully, as the party's guiding principles.

The Labour Party took even longer to establish itself as a major political party than the Liberals. Thirty-two years separated Keir Hardie's election in 1892 as one of the first two MPs to carry the Labour title and the formation of the first Labour Government by Ramsay MacDonald in 1924. In part that was because for a long time Labour had been seen, and had seen itself, not as a separate party in Parliament but simply as a group within the Liberal fold. Indeed, the Liberals had even looked down benignly on the baby which was eventually to outgrow them and had helped it on its way. A secret pact drawn up in 1903 by MacDonald and W. E. Gladstone's son, Herbert, the Liberal Chief Whip, provided for a straight Labour – Conservative fight in several constituencies, with the Liberals standing down in some in return for the support of the Labour Representation Committee in others. As a direct result of the pact, twenty-nine MPs were elected in 1906 who formed a group which, for the first time, called itself the Labour Party.

It was not until after the First World War that the Labour Party finally took off and began seriously to threaten the Liberals. For this the senior party was again responsible. During the war the Liberal Party had become split, on both ideological and personal grounds, between the supporters of David Lloyd George and Herbert Asquith. The divisions persisted after the war, with rival groups of Liberal candidates standing in both the 1918 and the 1922 election. In the latter election, for the first time, Labour became the main opposition to the Conservatives, with 142 MPs against a combined Liberal total of 115.

This brief sketch of the birth of the Liberal and Labour parties reveals some significant similarities in the origins and early development of the two most enduring new features of the British party system in the last 150 years. Both arose partly from a split within an existing party and partly from widespread dissatisfaction with the existing political system in the country as a whole. To that extent, there are clear parallels with the birth of the SDP. However, two other important elements in the establishment of the Liberal and Labour parties are not, so far at least, available to the SDP. It does not have the benefit of a brand-new electorate created by the extension of the franchise, although it is conceivable that it may, at some stage in its development, have the equally considerable advantage of the introduction of proportional representation, which would have an effect on political representation scarcely less important than that of the Reform Acts of the nineteenth century. Nor does it have the help and support of one of the two big existing parties, as the Liberals had when they effectively allied with the Whigs or as Labour had in the 1903 pact. It is true that the SDP is likely to have the support of the existing third party, the Liberals, but that will not be quite the same.

Two other features of the births of the Liberal and Labour parties are relevant to an assessment of the prospects for the SDP. The first is the length of time which it took both those parties to establish themselves. On previous form, even if the SDP were to break the political mould and become a major party, it could well be the year 2000 before it does so. The second feature is the extent to which the births of both the Liberal and the Labour parties were the result of a coincidence of different factors, some occurring in the narrow world of Westminster and others the result of deep economic, social and intellectual changes that were taking place in the country and even the world at large.

If we turn to look briefly at some of the unsuccessful new political parties which have sprung up in Britain, we can see that they failed because they were not formed in response to such wider and deeper movements in society. They have tended to be groups born wholly in Westminster, without the grass-roots support that both the Liberal and Labour parties had from their inception. They have also tended to have a narrower political focus, to resemble single-issue parties more than coalition. Their lives have been short, and they have often served as vehicles for conveying dissidents from one of the major parties into the other one.

Those features were certainly apparent in the case of the biggest single breakaway movement in the Liberal Party during the nineteenth century, the Liberal Unionists. The overriding reason for the secession in 1886 of about a hundred Liberal MPs, under the leadership of Joseph Chamberlain, was their disagreement with Gladstone over the single issue of Home Rule for Ireland. Admittedly, the Liberal Unionists were also more generally worried about what they took to be the radicalism and anti-imperialism of Gladstonian Liberalism, but they were unable to offer an alternative political creed which was different from that provided by the Tories. In a sense, the secession of the Liberal Unionists marked the final severance of the remaining Whigs from the Liberal Party that they had helped to create. They found their true political home as they gradually drifted into the arms of the opposition, which welcomed them by taking as its full title the Conservative and Unionist Party.

It is a strange irony that the next two significant groups to break away from major parties should both have been led by the leaders of those parties into coalitions with the opposition against the wishes of most party members. Lloyd George led his coalition Liberals in to the 1918 election against a much larger number of candidates standing as 'free' or 'Asquithian' Liberals, who opposed his continuation of the war-time alliance with the Conservatives. In 1931 MacDonald similarly split the Labour Party when, with a number of Labour Cabinet colleagues, he formed a National Government with the Conservatives and Liberals. In the General Election that year he led a small number of National Labour candidates against a much greater number of Labour candidates opposed to the National Government.

More splits and breakaway groups occurred in 1931 than in any other year before or since. The atmosphere of the country was curiously like that of our own times: a severe economic crisis was coupled with high unemployment. MacDonald's attempts to solve the problems by forming a National Government split not only the Labour Party but the Liberals as well. No fewer than three separate Liberal groups stood in the General Election: those supporting the National Government, led by Sir John Simon; a small group of Independent Liberals, led by Lloyd George; and those representing the main party, led by Sir Herbert Samuel. The Liberal Nationals (as the first group became known) continued as a separate body, unopposed by both Conservatives and Liberals, until 1948, when they changed their name to the National Liberal Party and effectively merged with the Tories.

The 1931 General Election was also notable for the unsuccessful challenge mounted by another breakaway party, which was in several respects rather similar to the Social Democratic Party formed fifty years later. The New Party had been set up earlier in 1931 by five Labour MPs led by Sir Oswald Mosley, who wanted to fight unemployment by letting public-sector borrowing soar and by establishing a major programme of public works. By the time of the election the party had gained the support of another two MPs, one Conservative and one Liberal, although it had already lost the support of three of its original founders, including John Strachey. In the election it contested twenty-four seats but failed to win a single one. In 1932 Mosley renamed the party the British Union of Fascists.

Another group broke away from the Labour Party the following year, this time on the left wing. The Independent Labour Party, (ILP) which had been formed in 1893, was affiliated to the Labour Party. After its members had started voting against the 1929 Labour Government, however, it was disaffiliated in 1932. In the 1935 General Election seventeen ILP candidates stood, all against Labour candidates, but only four were successful. Three ILP MPs were returned in the 1945 election, but after the death of the party's leader, James Maxton, in 1946, they returned to the Labour Party.

In the half-century between the formation of Mosley's New Party and the creation of the SDP only one other significant breakaway party emerged. In 1942 Sir Richard Acland, Liberal MP for Barnstaple, founded the Common Wealth Party. Its immediate aim was to contest all by-elections in which a 'reactionary' candidate was in the field and was not being opposed by a Labour or Liberal candidate because of the war-time electoral truce. The party won three by-elections during the war, but only one of its twenty-three candidates in the 1945 General Election was successful, and he joined the Labour Party when the results were known, as did Acland, who returned to the Commons in 1947 as a Labour MP.

The memory of those 'traitors' who broke away from Labour has lingered long in the party, and it is not surprising that the formation of the SDP has prompted comparisons with earlier breakaway groups. More than one Labour stalwart has told me that he puts the 'Gang of Four' into the same category as Ramsay MacDonald and his colleagues, although no one has dared to apply to its members Clement Attlee's withering remark about the 1931 episode: 'There was, in fact, no split, but only the shedding of a few leaves from the top of the tree, with a few parasitic appendages. The trunk and the main branches weathered the storm.' However, in an article in *The Times* on the eve of the SDP's launch Eric Heffer had no inhibitions about quoting a remark made by Vera Brittain, Shirley Williams's mother, about Mosley's New Party. Its members, she had said, were 'of the aristocratic, advanced Tory type; progressives who don't like the smell of the proletariat'.[1]

In fact, the most striking feature of those who have broken away from the Liberal and Labour parties to form new parties is not their treachery but their failure. The overwhelming message of their experience is the strength of the adversarial two-party system. It is bolstered both by the British electoral system, which grossly under-represents small parties, and by the persistence of class-based attitudes which identify the two major parties with the two nations of working-class North and middle-class South. It is even reinforced by the layout of the House of Commons, where the benches are ranged opposite each other rather than being arranged in a circle, as in several other national legislatures. Until recently the two-party system has also been supported by the vast majority of the electorate.

From time to time politicians and others have talked of trying to break the adversarial system by creating a centre party. In the late nineteenth and early twentieth centuries interest in this particular idea was expressed primarily by Conservative politicians who were worried that their party might be abandoning its 'One Nation' approach. In the second half of this century the idea has tended to be pursued with most enthusiasm by the Liberal Party and by certain sections of the media.

The first modern politician to fly the centre party kite was Randolph Churchill, the quixotic exponent of Tory democracy. After resigning from Lord Salisbury's Government in 1886 because he felt it was not doing enough for the common people, he approached Joseph Chamberlain, who had just left the Liberals, about the possibility of forming a new centre party. Despite the obvious attraction of a party created by an alliance of the more democratically inclined Conservatives and the more radical Liberal Unionists, his initiative came to nothing. Other leading dissentient Liberals whom he approached showed no interest, while the reaction of the political establishment was summed up by Sir William Harcourt's remark that the new party would be 'all centre and no circumference'. During a stroll through Hyde Park in 1887, Churchill and Chamberlain agreed to bury their plans for a new party.

Chamberlain was involved in another, rather more half-hearted attempt to create a new centre party in about 1900. This time the proposal was for an alliance between the Liberal Unionists and the Liberal Imperialists led by Asquith and Lord Rosebery. However, personal relations between Chamberlain and the two Liberals were bad, and he ruined any chance that there might have been of a realignment of parties when he espoused tarriff reform in 1903 and united all Liberals against him in defence of free-trade principles.

Almost certainly, the most determined advocate of a centre party in the first half of the twentieth century was Lord Robert Cecil, later Viscount Cecil of Chelwood. Although by upbringing and temperament a High Church Tory, Cecil's Christian idealism inclined him towards views on many subjects – including women's suffrage, free trade and, above all, the importance of the League of Nations – which were closer to those of the Liberals or even of the Labour Party. He broke with the Conservatives in 1910 and resigned from Lloyd George's coalition Government in 1918. It was after his resignation that he launched his bid to form a new centre party.

Cecil was concerned that the Conservative Party had abandoned its traditional 'One Nation' approach in favour of a new, narrower commitment to capitalism. He was equally unhappy about the cynical opportunism which he saw lying at the heart of Lloyd George's coalition Government. What was needed, he felt, was a new centre party which would appeal to 'the non-political mass – the people who did not vote at the last election and those Conservatives who are not reactionary and passionately desire clean and honest government'. He saw the underlying policies of the new party as profit-sharing and co-partnership in industry, 'conciliation and union of classes at home, peace in Ireland, League of Nations foreign policy and, above all, economic sanity and retrenchment',[2] a mixture not altogether different from that offered by the SDP. However, he was unable to interest leading anti-Lloyd George Liberals like Asquith and Viscount Grey in his ideas and eventually returned to the Conservative fold in 1923, only to end up as a Labour supporter in the 1940s.

In the post-war period the idea of a new centre party has been periodically canvassed in the pages of certain newspapers and political weeklies. *The Times* regularly took up the theme. In 1948 the *Economist* ran a series of articles about the plight of the middle classes which toyed with the idea of a new centre party but rejected it as impractical. It wrote:

One can indeed imagine a simultaneous split in both Labour and Conservative ranks, a breakaway of liberals without the capital letter. . . . One can imagine; it is all good clean fun. But short of this most improbable consummation the prospects for a new centre party are nil.[3]

In the 1950s and 1960s the leading advocates of a realignment of British politics to produce a strong centre party were to be found in the Liberal Party. For many of its supporters, indeed, it was itself the centre party, providing a non-socialist alternative to the Conservatives and standing outside the adversarial battle between right and left. However, despite spectacular by-election successes like that in Orpington in 1962, the party could manage to return only a handful of MPs to Westminster and made little impact on the political life of the nation. It was clear that the emergence of a strong centre party would come about only if there were a split in the Labour and Tory ranks.

Jo Grimond, the Liberals' leader from 1956 to 1967, had high hopes that such a realignment might take place. He saw the Liberals as forming the nucleus of what he called a 'non-socialist radical party', which would be committed to such progressive policies as co-ownership in industry, the devolution of power from Westminster to the regions, the abandonment of Britain's defence role east of Suez and the country's entry into the EEC. He envisaged the new party taking substantial support from both Labour and the Conservatives

Grimond increasingly pinned his hopes on the prospect of a split in the Labour Party which, by the early 1960s, was bitterly divided over both unilateral nuclear disarmament and commitment to public ownership. He has written:

Our strategy depended upon the Labour Party or some part of it being convinced that, as a socialist party committed to public owner-ship of all the means of production, distribution and exchange, it had a poor future. The state of public opinion pointed to a realignment. There was a hope that the full-blooded socialists would split off to the Left leaving a radical party on the left of centre of British politics but free of socialist dogma.[4]

However, the split never came. The Labour party patched up its quarrels; the right won the battle over unilateralism, and the left retained Clause Four. After Gaitskell's sudden death the party leadership passed to the arch-conciliator Harold Wilson. The Liberals were forced to bury their hopes of a realignment. The prospect of forming a strong centre party seemed as remote as ever.

Several reasons are generally cited for the failure of the idea of a centre party to get off the ground in Britain. The first-past-the-post electoral system penalises third parties. The persistence of class division and prejudice reinforces adversarial politics and close identification with either Labour or Conservatives. The failure of past splits makes politicians in the two main parties particularly reluctant to break away. The most important reason of all, however, is associated with what is perhaps the central paradox of British politics. Although the two main parties are locked in a system which encourages confrontation and polarisation, they have both ardently pursued the same centre ground. Disraeli re-established the Conservatives as a credible party of government only when he adopted Peel's approach and jettisoned his commitment to protectionism. Subsequent leaders of both main parties have in practice similarly avoided doctrinaire policies and ideology, whatever language they have adopted in addressing the party faithful. That has been the secret of the survival of the two-party system.

This pursuit of a common centre ground was particularly marked in the thirty years following the Second World War. The outlook of successive Labour and Conservative Governments during that period was characterised by the description 'Butskellism', an amalgamation of the names of Gaitskell, the Labour leader, and R. A. Butler, Conservative Chancellor of the Exchequer from 1951 to 1955. Its main features were a strong commitment to political liberalism and representative democracy, a belief in the virtues of a mixed economy with flourishing private and public sectors and a desire to create a more equal society and to promote the general welfare of the community through a combination of redistributive taxation and high public expenditure.

Butskellism was a development of the political philosophy of social democracy which was first formulated in Britain in the writings of a remarkable group of progressive Liberal thinkers who were at their most productive and influential in the early years of the twentieth century. The New Liberals, as they were called, dissociated themselves from the *laissez-faire* doctrines, the extreme individualism and the hostility to the state that characterised some Victorian Liberals. Instead they developed a more constructionist philosophy, which stressed social rather than political reform and gave a positive role to the state.

The philisophy which they developed was distinct from both classical liberalism and pure socialism. Its most important and distinctive element was perhaps its stress on the idea of society as an ethical entity and a community which co-operated in public action for its own good. Some of the New Liberals, like J. A. Hobson and L. T. Hobhouse, who put the pursuit of liberty before the pursuit of equality, felt that this idea could best be achieved by appealing to the altruistic element in human nature and through voluntary means. They tended to remain in the Liberal Party. Others, like Graham Wallas and J. L. Hammond, who put the pursuit of equality first, believed that it could come only through the action of the state and were attracted into Fabian socialism and the Labour Party. In his recent book, *Liberals and Social Democrats*, Peter Clarke has distinguished the former as 'moral reformers' and the latter as 'mechanical reformers'.[5]

The principles of social democracy inspired much of the legislation of the Liberal Government of 1908 to 1915, including the introduction of old age pensions, a national insurance scheme and Lloyd George's famous People's Budget of 1911. In the 1930s they were further developed by two more great Liberal thinkers, William Beveridge and John Maynard Keynes, who introduced into social democratic thought a commitment to the welfare state and to full employment, both of which they believed could and should be achieved through a high level of public spending. Many of their ideas were implemented by the Labour Government elected in 1945 and consolidated and extended by the Conservative Governments of the 1950s.

It was difficult to see how any new party could establish itself as long as the Conservatives and Labour both clung to the principles of social democracy. This they did throughout the 1960s. In the succeeding decade, however, under the impact of economic crisis, faith in the common principles that had sustained the two-party system for so long began to wane, as did faith in that system itself. For the first time for sixty years a gap seemed to be opening in British politics for a third party to fill.

'Why don't you start your own party, Jim?'
(Evening Standard, *17 June 1980*)

CHAPTER 3

Changes in the 1970s

*Cracks in the two-party system, the impact of
Europe and the loss of faith in social democracy*

Presumably because of their training in the skill of picking
holes in an argument, lawyers have always constituted one of
the largest groups in the House of Commons. It is not surprising,
then, that the first special-interest group set up by the Social
Democratic Party should have been an association of lawyers.
Its inaugural meeting, held in the old hall of Lincoln's Inn on
29 April 1981, was addressed by Roy Jenkins, who chose to
offer his audience a fascinating analysis of the 1970s. His
observations serve as a suitable introduction to a survey of the
decade in which the origins of the new party lie.

'Throughout the decade of the 1970s', he began, 'I had the
increasing feeling that the times had become out of joint for
British politics.' As specific evidence for this assertion he pointed
to the progressive loosening of the grip of the two main parties
on the loyalty and enthusiasm of the electorate, their failure to
manage economic decline, the manifest unjustness of the electoral system, the increasingly damaging effects of adversarial
politics and the fact that divisions within the major parties
were becoming greater than those between them. Those factors, he said, had led him to the conclusion that the mould must
be broken and a new party created.

Of all those features of the 1970s, the failure to halt Britain's
economic decline was the most serious and of most concern to
the public as a whole. Inflation, falling productivity, balance-
of-payments crises and rising unemployment were recurrent
themes throughout the decade. They were, of course, aspects
of a worldwide recession which followed the quadrupling of
oil prices in the mid-1970s. But Britain seemed to suffer far
more than other Western countries, and her problems seemed
more deep-seated and more resistant to solution. Try as they

might, successive Labour and Conservative Governments failed to break the cycle of decline.

That failure was probably the major factor that contributed to the loss of faith in the political system which took place in the 1970s. As people saw Governments failing to get to grips with inflation, they became cynical about the efficacy of politicians and turned to other instruments for advancement and protection. There were several indications of this trend. Turnout in General Elections fell from 84 per cent in 1950 to 72.8 per cent in 1974. Membership of trade unions, by contrast, increased dramatically. As industrial militancy increased, some commentators suggested that it was the unions rather than the elected politicians who were now running the country. Academics and newspaper leader writers declared that Britain was fast becoming ungovernable. Once again, as in the early 1930s, the cry went up from certain quarters for coalitions, Governments of national unity and even military intervention. Abroad, where there had once been respect for Britain's traditions of democracy and stability, there was now a morbid fascination with the British disease.

One of the most conspicious aspects of this general collapse of confidence in the existing political structure was a loss of faith in the two-party system. Between 1950 and 1970 the Conservative and Labour parties between them had never won less than 87.5 per cent of the votes cast in General Elections. In the 1951 and 1955 elections their combined share of the vote actually exceeded 96 per cent. In the two elections of 1974 it dropped to 75 per cent. Because of the fall in turnout, the proportion of the electorate as a whole voting for the two main parties declined even more markedly, from 80 per cent in 1951 to 54.7 per cent in 1974.

One reason for this turning away from both Labour and the Conservatives was a growing dissatisfaction with the results of adversarial politics. It seemed to many people that incoming Governments spent much of their time simply undoing what the last administration had done. Nationalisation was followed by denationalisation and then again by renationalisation. The succession of see-sawing policies, lurching first to the right and then to the left, came to be seen as a possible reason for Britain's chronic economic weakness. A growing number of industrialists began to talk of the need for less adversarial politics and for the development of agreed principles about the future direction of the economy which would produce a stable framework for investment and planning.

There were also deeper reasons for the reduction in popular support for the two main parties. Psephologists noticed a major change in Britain's electoral behaviour. Throughout the 1950s and 1960s the electorate had been divided into two solid blocks, one firmly committed to Labour and the other to the Tories. A relatively small number of floating voters alternated between them and determined the outcome of elections. In the 1970s, however, the blocks started breaking up as the electorate became far more volatile. Nearly a third of the population voted for different parties in the two elections of 1974. Traditional loyalties were clearly breaking down.

The main agent responsible for this change was almost certainly the weakening of class as a determinant of voting behaviour. In their important study *Political Change in Britain*,[1] first published in 1969, David Butler and Donald Stokes had suggested that the class basis of party allegiance was already beginning to decline in the 1960s. The general affluence of the post-war period, the decline of manual jobs and growth in white-collar employment, and the development of the service sector of the economy combined to blur old social divisions and to produce a less class-ridden society. As a result, the class-based parties became less popular.

By contrast, the Liberals, who were not seen as a party representing a particular class interest, significantly improved their share of the vote. In the February 1974 election they won more than 21 per cent of the vote in England. Yet although they were doing well in terms of votes, the Liberals still failed to pick up more than a handful of seats. Under a system of strict proportional representation their 6,000,000 votes in that election (19.3 per cent of the total UK vote) would have given them 122 MPs. As it was, the British first-past-the-post system gave them just fourteen.

As long as the great majority of the population supported one or other of the two major parties there was comparatively little concern about the manifest unfairness of the British electoral system. There had not even been a great outcry in 1951, when, for the first time this century, a party came to power after winning fewer votes in an election than its main opponent. When the same thing happened again in February 1974 (Labour won four more seats than the Conservatives, despite polling some 300,000 fewer votes), there was more concern, however. There was an additional reason for the electorate's loss of faith in the first-past-the-post system. Its great virtue was supposed to be that it produced clear working majorities for Governments and did not lead to hung Parliaments. Yet in both the 1974 elections it failed to achieve that object. Unfairness might perhaps be tolerated; inefficiency certainly could not be. A growing body of opinion, at both the influential and the popular level, began to question whether Britain's voting system really was the best.

The campaign for electoral reform was one of those movements mentioned by Roy Jenkins, in his talk to the Social Democratic lawyers, which united politicians from all parties. The National Committee for Electoral Reform was launched in June 1976 by a group which included Lord Houghton of Sowerby and Professor John Mackintosh, the MP for Berwick and East Lothian, on the Labour side, Lord Carr of Hadley for the Conservatives, David Steel for the Liberals and others, like Dick Taverne, who were outside the conventional party system. In general, Liberals were the keenest to change the electoral system, although there was a certain amount of support for the idea in the Conservative Party. Labour had the fewest believers in proportional representation, although there were exceptions, including Brian Walden, the MP for Birmingham, Ladywood, and Anthony Lester, QC, a prominent Labour lawyer.

There was another, much bigger cause which united politicians from all three main parties in the 1970s and which produced far deeper divisions within parties than between them. It was, of course, Britain's membership of the EEC. That issue played a more important role than any other in bringing together the people who were to found the SDP. Tony Benn is right when he calls the SDP a Common Market party: it is just this, in three quite different ways. It was their battle over Europe within the Labour Party which first caused the founding members of the SDP to think seriously of splitting from the party. Their experience in the 1975 referendum campaign caused them to rethink their attitude to the two-party system and led them to see the possibility of new forms of political alignment. They also identify, more clearly than any other group of British politicians, with a specifically European style of politics. The battle within the Labour Party over Europe will be dealt with in the next chapter. In this chapter we are concerned with the impact that entry into the EEC had on Britain's politics in the 1970s, and specifically with its effect on the party system.

Apart from inflation, there is no doubt that EEC membership was the dominant political issue of the decade. It first surfaced with the publication in February 1970 of a White Paper on the costs and benefits of entry, following the assurance of the new French President, Georges Pompidou, that he would not veto Britain's attempt to join the EEC, as his predecessor, Charles de Gaulle, had done. The issue was still alive at the end of the decade, when the Labour Party Conference in November 1979 voted that Britain's continued membership of the Community should be reconsidered unless substantial changes were made in its structure. In between those two events a Conservative Government had taken Britain into the EEC, a Labour Government had renegotiated the terms of entry and, in 1975, the country had been faced with the constitutional innovation of a referendum on whether it wanted to stay in. It had decided by an overwhelming majority that it did. By the end of the 1970s, however, opinion polls suggested that there was a substantial majority in favour of Britain's withdrawal. It was not just in its party political allegiance that the British public was becoming more volatile.

The issue of Britain's membership of the EEC divided the two main parties. Although the Conservatives were generally in favour – their leader, Edward Heath, was a particularly ardent pro-European – a significant minority of back-benchers were opposed to entry, forty-one of whom actually voted against the Government in a division on 28 October 1971 on the principle of joining the EEC. The position of the Labour Party was more complicated. Although while he was Prime Minister Harold Wilson had enthusiastically applied for membership in 1967, and the Labour Party Manifesto for the 1970 General Election had been equally in favour, the party's mood changed after the election. It adopted a policy of opposition to Heath's terms of entry. However, a substantial minority of Labour MPs, including the deputy leader of the party, Roy Jenkins, remained committed to membership. Sixty-nine of them defied a three-line whip and voted with the Conservative Government in the crucial vote in October 1971.

Largely to placate the anti-EEC majority in the party, in 1972 Harold Wilson agreed to hold a referendum on Britain's continued membership within twelve months of Labour's return to power. The party fought the two elections of 1974 on a manifesto which included an undertaking to renegotiate the terms of membership and then to hold a referendum. The renegotiation, which was carried out by the Foreign Secretary, James Callaghan, was completed in March 1975, and the referendum was fixed for 5 June.

The public campaign fought between pro- and anti-Marketeers in the two months before the 1975 referendum was one of the most curious episodes in modern British politics. Both sides were given public money to produce pamphlets setting out their contradictory cases, while the Government produced a pamphlet of its own supporting the principle of continued membership. The two sides were vastly unequal in terms of their resources. Britain in Europe, the umbrella group for the pros, had extensive backing from industry and the City and established expensive headquarters both in Whitehall and just off Park Lane. The National Referendum Campaign, by contrast, had virtually no money and operated from two small-ish rooms off the Strand.

It was while they were campaigning for a yes vote in the referendum under the umbrella of Britain in Europe that Labour pro-Marketeers found that on this issue at least they had more in common with their political opponents than with many in their own party. In fact, several of them had been involved in an all-party campaigning organisation for some time. In June 1972 four leading Labour enthusiasts for the EEC – Roy Jenkins, Harold Lever, MP for Manchester, Cheetham, George Thomson, MP for Dundee East, and Tom Bradley, a former railway clerk and prominent moderate member of the NEC – who were worried about the anti-European drift in the party, had joined the European League for Economic Co-

Operation, an organisation which also included leading Conservative pro-Marketeers like Geoffrey Rippon and Douglas Hurd. Shortly afterwards three of the most active pro-Market Labour back-benchers – Dickson Mabon, MP for the Scottish constituency of Greenock, John Roper, MP for Farnworth, near Manchester, and David Marquand, who represented the Nottinghamshire mining constituency of Ashfield – were also co-opted into the League.

Britain in Europe developed out of the League. The structure of the new umbrella organisation was first worked out in September 1974 in a paper produced by John Harris (later Lord Harris of Greenwich), who had been personal assistant to Hugh Gaitskell when Leader of the Opposition, special assistant to Roy Jenkins in the 1960s and part-time director of the League since 1972. William Rodgers, Minister of State for Defence and a leading Labour pro-Marketeer, was sounded out as a possible administrator of the new organisation, but he declined and the job went to Sir Con O'Neill, a retired diplomat, who opened the offices of Britain in Europe for business in January 1975. Roy Jenkins had privately agreed to become president, although he did not 'go public' until after the Cabinet had declared its view in March, and William Whitelaw acted as *de facto* deputy president. Shirley Williams was a vice-president, and Labour Party members on the steering committee included William Rodgers, Lord Harris, John Roper, Dickson Mabon and Ernest Wistrich, director of the European Movement.

Britain in Europe operated at two levels. It mounted all-party campaigns for a yes vote in the referendum, and senior politicians like Edward Heath, Roy Jenkins and Jeremy Thorpe, the Liberal leader, shared the same platform at public meetings across the country. It also acted as an umbrella for campaigns undertaken by individual parties. The Labour Campaign for Britain in Europe was launched in April 1975, with Shirley Williams as its president, Dickson Mabon as chairman and William Rodgers, David Marquand and John Roper on its committee. It had eighty-eight MPs, twenty-one peers and twenty-five union officials among its sponsors.

In the debates which raged across the country in the spring of 1975 it was their own political colleagues, like Michael

Foot, Peter Shore, Tony Benn and Barbara Castle, with whom the Labour pro-Marketeers most regularly crossed swords, and those whom they traditionally saw as their political enemies with whom they found themselves in agreement. The experience had a subtle effect on their feelings about the two-party system. As Roy Jenkins later put it, 'It made some of the divisions in politics seem a little artificial.'

Some of those involved on the Labour pro-EEC side in the referendum campaign even seemed to suggest that it had converted them to the idea of coalition politics. Lord George-Brown, the former Labour Foreign Secretary, said at one meeting that the country was now in a position for 'something different from party government'. In a speech in Leeds during the weekend before the referendum Reg Prentice, the Labour Secretary of State for Education, said:

The Common Market Campaign has united the majority of realistic and moderate politicians of all three political parties. It has been a refreshing experience for us to work together in a common cause. I believe our co-operation has been welcomed by millions of people throughout Britain, who have become fed up with the traditional party dogfight. We must not lose this spirit of unity after June 5.[2]

In fact, most of the Labour pro-Marketeers, when challenged on the point, quickly repudiated the idea that their experiences in the referendum campaign had led them to espouse coalition politics. Prentice denied that his speech was a call for a coalition when it was interpreted in that light by the press. When Shirley Williams was publicly tackled on the same theme by Tony Benn she replied, 'I have never wanted coalition. I have never talked about coalition, and I am not after coalition.'[3]

However, there could be no denying that the campaign had altered their political perceptions and loyalties. This change was probably most marked in the case of Roy Jenkins, who was already out of sympathy with the tenor of the 1974 Labour Government. Friends recall that he found the referendum campaign an invigorating and liberating experience, not least because it enabled him to taunt old opponents on the Labour left. This he did with most crushing effect ten days before the referendum, when he announced, 'I find it increasingly difficult to take Mr Benn seriously as an economics

Minister.' Others also found that their debates with Labour anti-Marketeers had revealed fundamental disagreements about many matters apart from Europe. For them too it was a refreshing experience to be able to champion a cause in which they passionately believed and to find that there was a sizeable body of opinion in the country that shared their enthusiasm. When they came down off the platform and stayed behind after their meetings for a drink or a chat, they found that many of those people who would be voting yes for Europe were also profoundly disillusioned with the Labour Party and eager for a shake-up in the two-party system.

Seen in retrospect, entry into Europe may well prove to have had a similarly cataclysmic effect on British politics in the 1970s and 1980s to that of the repeal of the Corn Laws in the 1840s and 1850s and of Irish Home Rule in the 1880s and 1890s. Just as Peel's action in 1846 split the Tories and led directly to the founding of the Liberal Party, and Gladstone's single-minded pursuit of the Irish question gravely weakened the appeal of the Liberals, so the debate about Britain's membership of the EEC has already split the Labour Party and has provoked the formation of the SDP. The issue of Europe has had a peculiarly powerful effect in distancing several leading politicians from their own parties (just how powerful, in the case of social democrats in the Labour Party, we shall see in the next chapter). Roy Jenkins, the first British President of the European Commission, literally distanced himself from the Labour Party, a four-year self-imposed exile in Brussels serving as a prelude to his new career with the Social Democrats. In their very different ways, Enoch Powell and Edward Heath both became alienated from the Conservative Party because of their strong feelings about the issue of the EEC.

There was another, quite different way in which entry into Europe changed the perceptions of British politicians in the 1970s. It brought them into close contact with a system of politics which, in several important respects, was quite unlike their own. None of the other eight countries in the EEC had a simple two-party system, and most of them practised coalition politics. They all used a system of proportional representation for their elections. Their political parties were funded by the state rather than through trade union and private corporate donations. Most of them had a wide measure of devolution, and in some cases a federal system of government. In political and constitutional respects, Britain was the odd man out.

The outlook and style of the main political parties in the EEC were also markedly different from those of the three major parties in Britain. British Conservatives elected to the European Parliament did not sit with the large Christian Democrat group, as might have been expected, but rather formed their own group with a handful of Danish Conservatives. Although the British Liberal Party affiliated to the Liberal and Democratic group, there was some disquiet about the right-wing bias of some of its bedfellows there. Superficially, the Labour Party did not appear to experience the same difficulties over fitting into the European political scene. Every country in the EEC had a socialist party, and the Labour Party was already linked with all of them through its membership of Socialist International. The strong socialist group in the European Parliament was the obvious home for British Labour Party delegates.

In reality, however, there were considerable differences of policy and outlook between the Labour Party and the other socialist parties of the EEC. The most obvious lay in attitudes to the Community itself. The Labour Party stood alone in not favouring closer European integration and in having so many anti-Marketeers within its ranks. There were other less obvious but more fundamental differences, which derived largely from historical factors. While the British party, as its name implied, had its roots in working-class consciousness and the trade union movement, the Continental parties had more distinct ideological origins and perspectives. In France and Italy the socialist parties had to compete with significant Communist parties. In Germany and Denmark, the EEC countries most similar to Britain in many respects, their names signified their adherence to the philosophy of social democracy.

In its origins European social democracy was uncompromisingly Marxist, much more so than British socialism. Both the West German SPD and the Danish Socialdemokrater, for example, grew directly out of the First International, held under Marx's influence in 1864. However, following the Russian Revolution they became progressively more liberal and anti-Communist, stressing the democratic aspects of their philosophy and playing down socialism in practice, if not always in theory. By the 1930s social democracy in Europe was coming to mean support for parliamentary democracy and for the mixed economy.

The continuing process of liberalisation which took place in the post-war period can be seen particularly clearly in the case of the West German SPD, by far the largest of the social democratic parties of Europe. Although by the late 1940s and early 1950s it was effectively a moderate, reformist party, it was performing badly in elections. A growing element in the SDP, made up chiefly of local burgomasters and led by Willy Brandt and Helmut Schmidt, attributed this lack of electoral success to the party's Marxist image. At the Bad Godesberg conference in 1959 they succeeded in persuading the SPD finally to sever its links with its Communist past and to drop its ideological commitment to full public ownership. The party abandoned its traditional anti-clericalism and openly accepted the benefits of the mixed economy and the profit motive. Its election performance improved dramatically. Before Bad Godesberg the party's share of the vote had hovered around 30 per cent. It rose to 36 per cent in 1961 and to 40 per cent in 1969, since when it has consistently been the senior partner in coalitions governing the country.

This aspect of European social democracy could not fail to strike British Labour politicians, contrasting as it did with their own party's continuing commitment to nationalisation through Clause Four of its constitution. Nor was it only the socialist parties of the countries in the EEC that had abandoned that commitment. In a lecture in Costa Rica in 1975 on the subject of social democracy in Europe, the late Anthony Crosland pointed out that neither the Swedish nor the Austrian social democratic parties had made more than passing references to the subject in their latest programmes. He concluded: 'Amongst the European socialist parties, the British Labour Party is unique in the doctrinal energy which it still devotes to the issue of public ownership.'[4]

The British encounter with Europe, and with European social democracy in particular, also had much wider effects. It helped to shape a new consensus which was already forming in the country as a result of economic, social and intellectual changes as far-reaching as those which had led to the awakening of liberalism in the middle of the nineteenth century and to the growth of a collectivist mentality at the dawning of the twentieth century. If the bourgeoisie created by the Industrial Revolution was the harbinger of the first movement, and the proletariat created as a result of mass production and the factory system the standard bearer of the second, then those who rode on the crest of this third great wave of Western thought were the products of the newly emerging post-industrial society. They were, typically, journalists, economists, educators, communicators, scientists and all those others who worked in what the American sociologist Daniel Bell has called the new 'intellectual technology'.

It was the members of this new class who built the new political consensus which began to emerge in the 1970s. Their gurus were E. F. Schumacher, Fred Hirsch and Ivan Illich; their daily Bible was the *Guardian* newspaper; their creed was a pot-pourri of 'small is beautiful', concern for the environment and the quality of life, community involvement and self-help, decentralisation and anti-corporatism, industrial democracy and co-operation rather than confrontation in industry. They wanted to save the whale, to preserve village schools and to see Britain adopt a style of politics which was much closer to that of Europe. They didn't much like the power of the trade unions, made equally nasty noises about multinational companies, and faceless bureaucrats in the Civil Service and complained frequently about the deteriorating quality and remoteness of the public education, health and welfare services.

In many ways the emergence of this new mood was a sign of the loss of faith in the old social democratic consensus which had formerly prevailed among opinion formers and which had effectively ruled the country since 1945. At one level faith in social democracy collapsed in the 1970s simply because it was associated with economic failure. The period in which it had been the dominant creed of Governments had also been the one in which the British economy had declined at an accelerating rate. By the mid-1970s social democracy could no longer deliver the goods. Inflation and unemployment were rising simultaneously, and the economic growth which was regarded as the precondition for greater equality and welfare in society was simply no longer there.

There were other, less immediate reasons for the collapse of confidence in social democracy. The welfare state, its most distinctive and once its proudest creation, seemed to have turned sour and to have become overburdened by bureaucracy and red tape. Hospitals seemed increasingly to be run for the benefit of administrators rather than patients, comprehensive schools to be soulless jungles far removed from the humane and idealistic visions of their founders. Parliamentary democracy seemed less and less effective as powerful vested interests rode roughshod over the wishes of the people and their elected representatives. Government by consent seemed to involve capitulating to corporate interests and letting the trade unions determine the policy of the country. Above all, perhaps, there was a growing feeling that the state had ceased to be the servant of society and had become its master.

Not everyone felt this way. Among the older members of the working classes there was still much faith in social democracy and its principles and much gratitude for the health service, the bus pass and the pension. But in general there was evidence that the population as a whole was beginning to share the feelings of the new intelligentsia. Polls showed that the main issues of public concern were inflation, trade unions and the quality of life. In the 1960s they had been social welfare, pensions, health and housing.

Both major parties responded to, and reflected, the national loss of faith in social democracy. The Conservatives did so first and most completely. With the election of Margaret Thatcher as leader in 1975, the party apparently turned its back on the 'One Nation' tradition of Harold Macmillan, R. A. Butler and Iain Macleod. Out went a Keynsian commitment to full employment and a Beveridgite belief in an expanding welfare state. Instead there was a revival of nineteenth-century notions of *laissez-faire* and self-help, a promise to roll back the frontiers of the state, to reduce public spending drastically and to encourage individual initiative. No longer would government be a cosy matter of social contracts and bargaining with the unions; no longer either would a Government spend its way out of a recession.

Labour moved away much more slowly and cautiously from its old social democratic principles. They were still to the fore when James Callaghan took the party into the 1979 General Election. But a growing body of opinion in the party, led by Tony Benn, was demanding much more full-blooded socialism, with the nationalisation of leading companies, workers' control of their firms, import controls and withdrawal from the EEC. A new and more strident class-consciousness was emerging in the party to challenge the soft social democratic consensus that had dominated it for so long.

The victory of Mrs Thatcher in the 1979 election appeared to confirm the electorate's rejection of social democratic politics. In other ways that election result seemed to be a reversal of the trends of the 1970s. It produced a clear result and an apparent vote of confidence in the two-party system: more than 80 per cent of those who voted supported either Labour or the Conservatives. The volatility of the mid-1970s had apparently evaporated; the country had once again polarised into two blocks, the working-class North, more solidly Labour than ever, and the prosperous South, more determinedly Tory.

Yet the message of the election was not as simple as that. Other evidence suggests that it did, in fact, mark a further stage in the progressive loss of faith in the two-party system which had been apparent throughout the past two decades. When electors coming out of the polling stations after voting in the 1964 election were asked whether they identified strongly with either the Conservative or the Labour party, 40 per cent replied in the affirmative. When the same question was asked in 1979, the proportion identifying strongly with either of the two main parties had halved to 20 per cent. Moreover, turnout in 1979 was lower than in the February 1974 election, and only 61 per cent of all those eligible to vote had supported one of the two main parties.

The findings of opinion polls measuring support for the creation of a new centre party at the beginning and end of the decade are more difficult to assess. In September 1972 a poll undertaken by Opinion Research Centre for *The Times* found that 35 per cent of the population felt either 'very strongly' or 'fairly strongly' that they would vote for a 'left-of-centre' centre party formed by a Liberal alliance with well-known Labour Party moderates like Roy Jenkins, Shirley Williams, George Thomson and Harold Lever. The poll showed that even more people (40 per cent) said that they would support a centre party formed by a Liberal alliance with moderate members of the Conservative Party.

A similar poll carried out for *The Times* by Opinion Research and Communication in January 1980 found that 55 per cent of the electorate wanted to see a new party formed in the centre of British politics. However, there was widespread disagreement over what its constituent parts should be. Only 23 per cent of respondents said that they would vote for the candidate of a centre party formed by moderate and right-wing members of the Labour Party and Liberals, and even fewer (16 per cent) said that they would support a centre party formed solely of Labour moderates who had split away from the left.

Answers to other questions in those two polls suggested that dissatisfaction with the prevailing political system had remained at a fairly constant (and high) level throughout the decade. Exactly the same number of people (53 per cent) agreed that the present party political system no longer worked properly. A slightly smaller proportion in 1980 (55 per cent) than in 1972 (60 per cent) agreed that people who did not want to support either the Labour or the Conservative party had no opportunity to make their views heard, but a larger proportion (75 per cent in 1980, compared with 70 per cent in 1972) agreed that the trade unions had too much power over the Labour Party.[5]

The overall message of Britain's traumatic experiences in the 1970s is a confusing one. The election at the end of the decade had apparently signalled a return by the country to the two-party system of politics which it had earlier seemed to be rejecting. Yet other indicators suggested that fewer people than ever before identified closely with the two main parties. Traditional class-based loyalties were breaking down, and the electorate was becoming more volatile, but the 1979 election suggested that the nation was more divided than ever between the haves and the have-nots.

The one clear message seemed to be that faith in social democracy, as preached and practised in Britain by both major parties since the war, had broken down. At the same time there was increasing interest in the very different kind of social democracy found in many of the countries of Western Europe and in a political and economic system which would put more emphasis on individual freedom, voluntary and co-operative association, decentralisation and conservation of the environment. A new class was emerging in Britain which could perhaps form the basis of a realignment of politics as significant as that produced by the emergence of the manufacturing and commercial middle classes in the mid-nineteenth century and of the collectivised proletariat in the early twentieth century.

Within this new class, and within the electorate as a whole, there was widespread potential support for a new centre party which would stand outside the traditional Labour and Conservative dogfight. Many people had found the pact between the Labour and Liberal parties between March 1977 and the autumn of 1978 a refreshing and welcome break from the politics of confrontation. The *Times* poll of January 1980 found that 60 per cent of the population considered that the Labour Party had moved too far to the left and 46 per cent that the Conservatives had moved too far to the right. The centre ground was still clearly very attractive to the electorate as a whole. The Conservatives had chosen to desert it. Much depended on whether Labour followed suit.

(The Times, *13 January 1981*)

CHAPTER 4

The Transformation of the Labour Party

The social democrats lose control

The British Labour Party has always been an uneasy coalition of fundamentally different interests and groups. It was born of a strange alliance between working-class trade unionists and middle-class socialist intellectuals. It has never since been able to decide whether it is a party of gradual reform in the liberal and social democratic tradition or of red-hot, full-blooded socialism.

The history of the Labour Party has essentially been one of struggle between socialists and social democrats to commit the party to their own particular views. A general pattern has emerged: the party has moved leftwards while in Opposition but has returned to the centre ground of social democracy in Government. Formerly, compromise tended to prevail, with the social democrats firmly ensconced in the main positions of power and the socialists making bold pronouncements of policy which had no chance of being implemented. Over the last fifteen years or so, however, this balance has changed, at first gradually and almost imperceptibly, but then with a gathering momentum and increasingly obvious effect. Each leftward lurch has become more difficult to check than the last. Fed up with their impotence and with what they saw as the capitulation of successive Labour Governments to the forces of capitalism and conservatism, the socialists have set about taking over positions of power and influence at every level of the party. As a result, the social democrats have gradually lost control.

The heyday of social democratic influence and control was, strangely enough, during the years of Opposition between 1955 and 1963. Hugh Gaitskell, who led the party during this period, was more firmly in the social democrats' camp than any Labour leader before or since. He was supported by a powerful body of loyal, right-wing trade union leaders and an impressive group of 'revisionist' intellectuals led by Anthony Crosland.

Crosland's book *The Future of Socialism*,[1] was the fullest and most influential expression of the philosophy of the Gaitskellite Labour Party. It built on the ideas of Keynes and Beveridge, being wholly committed to the goals of full employment and the extension of the welfare state. It established the pursuit of equality as the most important task of a Labour Government but insisted at the same time on the preservation of personal freedom and adherence to the principles of representative democracy. Most important of all, perhaps, it argued that nationalisation should no longer be seen as the principal objective of a modern social democratic state. Rather, a Labour Government should concentrate on running a successful mixed economy which could generate the high growth needed to sustain increased public expenditure.

The last part of this new creed was the one which stuck most in the throats of the socialists in the party, as Gaitskell found when he tried to have it officially embodied in the party's constitution. Influenced by the example of the German SPD at Bad Godesberg a few months earlier, he proposed in his speech at the two-day conference which followed Labour's defeat in the 1959 election that the party should drop Clause Four of its constitution and so abandon its formal commitment to public ownership.

Gaitskell badly miscalculated the response to his proposal from the party as a whole. On the left it provoked a predictable howl of protest. However, many moderate trade union leaders also gave it a cool reception. They saw no need to change the constitution in a way that would provoke serious disunity in the party and preferred to preserve the present ambiguity whereby Labour was in practice committed to a mixed economy but still managed to keep the purists happy by remaining nominally attached to public ownership. Not for the first or the last time, those counselling compromise and fudging won the day, and Gaitskell's proposal was quietly dropped.

At the Labour Party Conference in Scarborough the following year Gaitskell suffered a more serious defeat when the party's official policy of multinational nuclear disarmament was rejected in favour of unilateralism. In a defiant speech he promised to 'fight and fight and fight again' to reverse the decision and also indicated that neither the leadership nor the Parliamentary Labour Party (PLP) would feel itself bound by the vote. This was a direct challenge to the widely accepted view that Conference should be the supreme voice in the determination of Labour Party policy.

The issues that were raised in the Conferences of 1959 and 1960 – whether Labour was a socialist party committed to nationalisation or a social democratic party believing in a mixed economy, whether or not it supported unilateralism, and the respective roles of Conference, the leadership and the PLP in the formulation of policy – were to resurface again in almost exactly the same form twenty years later. The difference was that while in 1960 the social democrats had the resources and the will to fight back and reverse their defeats by the left, in 1980 they lacked both.

The setbacks suffered by Gaitskell in the 1959 and 1960 Conferences led a number of social democrats to set up their own campaigning group within the party. In the past only the left had gone in for such intra-party organisations, the best-known being the Keep Left group which had been set up in the 1940s. However, some of those on the right of the party now considered that the situation was potentially so serious that they came together in the summer of 1960 and agreed to draw up a manifesto and to issue a rallying cry to moderates. In the words of one of them, Dick Taverne, then a bright young lawyer and prospective Parliamentary candidate:

We were determined to make one last effort to prevent the Party becoming a neo-Marxist Party dedicated to large-scale nationalisation at home and neutralism abroad, a Party without hope of capturing power except in the event of a national catastrophe.[2]

The Campaign for Democratic Socialism was formally launched immediately after the 1960 Scarborough Conference. Its leading members were a group of young social democrats who had Parliamentary ambitions but had not yet been elected as MPs. Prominent among them were Brian Walden (like Taverne, a former office-holder in the Oxford Union) and Denis Howell who, like Walden, came from a Midlands working-class background. Taverne became treasurer of the Campaign, and William Rodgers was recruited from the Fabian Society as full-time organiser. Shirley Williams, who had succeeded Rodgers as secretary of the Fabians, was sympathetic to the aims of the Campaign but deemed it wise, in view of her new job, not to become involved.

The Campaign achieved considerable success. Its lobbying of trade unions helped to secure a defeat for unilateralism at the 1961 Party Conference. It also organised support for the selection of social democrats as Parliamentary candidates. The Campaign was dissolved in 1963, its task having apparently been accomplished. By then Dick Taverne, William Rodgers and Denis Howell had become MPs. Shirley Williams and Brian Walden were to follow them into the Commons the following year.

The bonds which participation in the Campaign for Democratic Socialism had forged among this group of young Labour social democrats remained strong for many years. They met regularly for dinners which, in the words of Taverne, 'were rather like regimental reunions, with recollections of the glorious battles of past campaigns'.[3] They also continued to feel that sense of almost conspiratorial comradeship which belongs to those, more usually on the political left, who form a 'party within a party'.

When Gaitskell died in January 1963, social democrats were firmly in control of all the major organs of the Labour Party, including the National Executive Committee (NEC), the PLP and the Conference. In the contest to decide the succession, however, the social democrat candidate, George Brown, lost to Harold Wilson, who was, ostensibly at least, a man of the left. The reasons for this were essentially personal. A substantial number of middle-of-the-road and right-wing Labour MPs doubted Brown's capacity for leadership and opted for Wilson.

On the face of it, Wilson's election as leader did not alter the balance of the party. Preaching his own brand of revisionist socialism, which put more stress on the white heat of technology than on the old nostrum of public ownership, he led Labour into a triumphant victory in the 1964 election and so launched a period during which the party was in power for eleven of the next fifteen years. The style of his Government was firmly non-ideological and pragmatic, and its dominant figures, George Brown, Roy Jenkins, James Callaghan, Anthony Crosland and Denis Healey, were all unmistakably in the social democratic tradition.

In a deeper sense, however, Wilson's election as leader and the 1964 General Election victory marked the start of the decline of social democracy in the Labour Party. His Government succeeded in alienating left and right alike, which led to the internal feuding and bickering that has gone on ever since. This was partly due to a failure to satisfy ambitious expectations which had been built up in the thirteen 'wasted years' of Conservative rule and could not be fulfilled in the adverse economic climate of the late 1960s. But it was also the result of a style of leadership which was based on the compromise and the fudge. Quite possibly, that was the only way of keeping such a disparate party together at a time of acute economic crisis, but it left a legacy of bitterness and frustration which eventually boiled over at the beginning of the 1980s.

Three separate difficulties afflicted the Labour Party in the decade between 1964 and 1974: a decline in its vote and membership, the disaffection of the left and the disaffection of the right. All three factors are interrelated, and together they help to explain why the party became an increasingly unhappy place for social democrats.

In 1951 Labour had won 48.8 per cent of the vote, its highest proportion ever in a General Election. The figure dropped steadily through the 1950s, and even in its 1964 victory the Labour Party was able to poll only 44.1 per cent. Although its share of the vote rose in 1966, it fell back to 43.1 per cent in 1970 and dropped to 37.2 per cent in February 1974, its lowest since 1931. The statistics for individual membership of the party illustrated a similar story. In the early 1950s there had been well over a million paid-up members. By 1964 the figure was down to 830,000; by 1970 it had dropped to 775,693 and by 1974 to 691,889.

The decline both in the party's vote and in its membership was partly a consequence of the social changes noted in Chapter 3. Class-based patterns of voting were becoming less marked, and Labour was hit particularly hard by the steady erosion of its traditional manual working-class base as manufacturing contracted and the service and 'white-collar' sectors of the economy expanded. A growing cynicism about politics also played a part, particularly in the decline in membership. Many idealistic and vigorous young people who in previous decades would have joined the Labour Party now devoted their energies to such organisations as Oxfam and Shelter, which they felt were more beneficial to society.

Not only the size but also the composition of the party's membership was changing. During the 1960s and 1970s Labour fell victim to the so-called process of 'embourgeoisement' so beloved of sociologists studying those decades. The party was quite simply taken over by the middle classes. This happened at all levels, inside Parliament and within the trade union section as well as among the general membership in the country.

The embourgeoisement of the PLP was particularly striking. In 1945 39.2 per cent of the newly elected Labour MPs were from working-class backgrounds. By October 1974 the proportion had fallen to just 4.6 per cent. Teachers and lawyers took over from miners and steelworkers as the biggest occupational groups in the PLP. As Collin Mellors has put it in his fascinating study *The British MP*, the 'men of ideas' had replaced the 'men of toil'.[4] Within the trade union movement there was a double process of embourgeoisement. First, white-collar unions representing the increasing numbers employed in clerical, administrative and service jobs grew to challenge the traditional dominance of blue-collar unions representing manual workers. Secondly, union general secretaries and officers, many of whom played a dominant role in relations with the Labour Party, were increasingly recruited from the ranks of university and polytechnic graduates rather than from among those working their way up from the shop floor.

It was in the ordinary constituency Labour parties up and down the country, however, that the take-over of the middle classes was most thorough. Young graduates, fresh from reading politics or social science at university or polytechnic, joined their local Labour party, often in a working-class area that was being 'gentrified' by the influx of professional people and owner-occupiers. Sometimes they deliberately rented bedsitters in run-down areas which were traditional Labour strongholds. Gradually, assisted by their greater articulateness and organisational abilities, they ousted old working-class activists from their positions as branch and ward officers.

The effect of this middle-class take-over might be expected to have helped the cause of social democracy rather than that of the socialist left. Yet it had precisely the reverse effect. Socialism in Britain has traditionally been a peculiarly middle-class enthusiasm. In the early days of the Labour Party it was the bourgeois elements in the Social Democratic Federation and the Fabian Society that preached the socialist gospel to a generally less than enthusiastic trade union movement. George Orwell had observed in 1948: 'It is only the middle class that thinks in revolutionary terms.'[5] It was significant that throughout the 1960s and early 1970s the most left-wing of the leading figures in the party, Michael Foot and Tony Benn, were also the most middle-class in their background, while those on the right, like George Brown, Ray Gunter and Bob Mellish, tended to be from the working classes. The meritocrats from the lower middle classes, Wilson, Callaghan and Healey, stayed roughly in the middle.

The new bourgeois recruits to the Labour Party had been radicalised by their experiences of higher education. They belonged to the generation of student protest, of demonstrations against Vietnam and in favour of easier abortion, and of teach-ins on Marxism and revolutionary theory. Their outlook was wholly different from that of the working-class stalwarts who had traditionally dominated local Labour parties. A recent study which asked representatives of the two groups why they were involved in local politics found that the former were much more likely to reply, 'To pursue socialist goals', and the latter to say, 'To help people.'[6]

These new recruits were bitterly disillusioned by the performance of the Labour Governments of 1964 to 1970. They regarded Wilson and his Cabinet colleagues as having abandoned the principles of socialism in favour of a kind of pale pink Toryism. They set about trying to radicalise the party in a number of ways – by moving Conference resolutions bitterly critical of the Government's actions, by trying to apply more pressure to MPs to campaign for socialist measures, and by consolidating their hold over the vital organs of the party, first at local and then at national level, so that they could gain more influence and control.

The consequences of these activities, all of which were perfectly legitimate, were devastating. They destroyed the fraternal, loyalist atmosphere in which the Labour Party had normally conducted its internal affairs even at times of serious dissension, as in 1960. It was virtually unheard of for Conference to pass resolutions critical of Labour Governments, for example, but that was what started happening regularly after 1966, as the radical delegates from the constituencies were joined by a new, more left-wing group of trade union leaders. It had also been very rare for Labour MPs to find themselves under pressure from their constituency parties. Indeed, the traditional attitude of most local parties towards their MPs had been one approaching idolisation. Increasingly, however, MPs were finding themselves confronted at general management committee meetings by highly articulate and rather hostile party members demanding to know why they were supporting a capitalist Government. Lengthy debates on spending cuts and alternative economic strategies, often lasting far into the night, replaced the traditionally rather short meetings of many local parties, which had often adjourned to the pub at a reasonably early hour for a 'social' or a gossip.

The social democrats, whose numbers were also swollen by the new middle-class recruits to Labour, though to a much less considerable and less conspicuous extent, were also disillusioned by the performance of the Wilson Governments. If the left was worried by the abandonment of socialism, they were disappointed by the absence of vision and purpose. In 1967 a pamphlet on this theme appeared under the title *Change Gear*. Its authors were David Marquand and John Mackintosh, two distinguished intellectuals in the Croslandite tradition, and David Owen, a bright young doctor. All three had been elected to Parliament the previous year. They argued for more social expenditure, the devaluation of the pound and radical measures of constitutional reform which would give Parliament more control over the bureaucracy and would establish elected assemblies in Scotland, Wales and the English regions. The leadership's brusque rejection of their proposals caused them considerable disappointment.

It was in the period of Opposition from 1970 to 1974, however, that many social democrats became most disillusioned with Wilson's leadership of the Labour Party. The issue which alienated them was the EEC, and in particular what they saw as Wilson's unprincipled and opportunistic changes of position, first on the terms of entry for Britain and second on the question of whether there should be a referendum on the subject.

Europe in general, and the EEC in particular, had long held a particularly high place in the affections of British social democrats. Anthony Crosland had favourably compared the political and social structures of the Scandinavian countries with those of Britain in *The Future of Socialism*. As early as 1959 an enthusiastic group of Labour pro-Europeans, led by Roy Jenkins, Norman Hart, a public relations executive, and Jack Diamond, MP for Gloucester, set up a Labour Common Market Committee to mobilise support in the party for British membership of the newly formed EEC. In the mid-1960s it changed its name to the Labour Committee for Europe and recruited the organisational skills of William Rodgers, fresh from his triumphs with the Campaign for Democratic Socialism.

There was one particular forum which helped to shape the pro-Europeanism of some of Labour's leading social democrats in the 1960s and also played a significant role in changing their attitudes to their own party. The annual conferences held at Königswinter on the River Rhine bring together leading members of the Labour Party and of the West German SPD, together with academics and journalists. Among those who attended most regularly on the British side throughout the 1960s were Roy Jenkins, Denis Healey, Shirley Williams and William Rodgers, while the German contingent was normally led by Willy Brandt and Helmut Schmidt.

Regular attenders at Königswinter (which, by a strange coincidence, is just across the river from Bad Godesberg) recall that the British Labour Party group was struck by an observation that was made more than once by its SPD counterparts. Brandt and Schmidt commented that they could not understand how it was that Britain apparently had two Labour parties. At Königswinter they met representatives of a party that was committed to NATO, the EEC and the mixed economy.

But when they went to meetings of the Socialist International they seemed to meet members of a totally different party, which was committed to unilateralism, withdrawal from Europe and further nationalisation.

Throughout the 1960s the Labour visitors to Königswinter had at least felt that their party as a whole was moving in broadly the same direction as the SPD, even if the attitudes of its left wing baffled their German hosts. In the early 1970s, however, they felt increasingly out of step. While the SPD was becoming more committed to the preservation and strengthening of the EEC, the Labour Party had adopted a policy of effective opposition to Britain's membership.

The importance of the EEC issue in forming the collective consciousness of the social democrats in the Labour Party was mentioned in Chapter 3. It is hard to exaggerate the camaraderie generated by their fight against the rest of the party on this issue. As in the Campaign for Democratic Socialism, but this time in Parliament, they operated as a party within a party, with William Rodgers acting as an unofficial whip for the sixty-nine pro-Market Labour MPs who voted with the Conservative Government in the vote on 28 October 1971 on the principle of membership.

The battle over Europe forged alliances among social democrats in the Labour Party which persisted right up to the breakaway from the party by some of them ten years later. Dick Taverne recalls a meeting of pro-Marketeers in his flat to discuss tactics as early as June 1970. Present were Roy Jenkins, the acknowledged leader of the group, George Thomson, who had laid the groundwork for Britain's application to join the EEC at the tail-end of the Wilson Government, Bill Rodgers, David Owen, David Marquand and others. Taverne writes: 'We feared not only that the Party would turn against the Market but that we might face a split as serious as that of 1960 over nuclear disarmament. Only this time the odds would be against the social democrats.'[7]

The issue provoked serious talk about a social democrat breakaway from the Labour Party. Taverne recalls that on the evening after the second reading of the European Communities Bill in November 1971, he and Bill Rodgers went to see Roy Jenkins in his London home and told him that they thought he should resign from the Labour deputy leadership and form a new social democratic party. 'Bill was just as hawkish as I was,' Taverne says, 'Roy decided that he needed to consult his supporters, and they told him not to split.'

In the event, Jenkins did resign from the deputy leadership the following April, after the Shadow Cabinet had performed a complete *volte face* on the issue of whether there should be a referendum on Britain's continued membership of the EEC. Two weeks after rejecting Tony Benn's proposal for a referendum, the Shadow Cabinet decided to accept it. This action also provoked the resignations of George Thomson, Harold Lever, David Owen and Dick Taverne. After considerable agonising, Shirley Williams decided to stay in the Shadow Cabinet.

Although there does not appear to have been any more talk about splitting from the party at this stage, the pro-Marketeers' anger and frustration with the Labour leadership mounted in 1973 and 1974. By the time of the October 1974 General Election campaign Europe had become, for several of them, an issue which they regarded as more important than their continued membership of the Labour Party. During the campaign Shirley Williams said that she would not remain in active politics if Britain left the EEC, and Roy Jenkins made it clear that he would not stay in a Cabinet which had to carry out withdrawal.

Europe was one of several issues over which a number of social democrat Labour MPs clashed with their local constituency parties in the early 1970s. The first to encounter serious trouble was Dick Taverne, the former treasurer of the Campaign for Democratic Socialism. Ever since his election as MP for Lincoln in a by-election in 1962 he had enjoyed an uneasy relationship with left-wingers in the local party, who regarded him as Gaitskellite who had been foisted on them by the leadership. During the period of Labour Government from 1964 to 1970 there were no serious clashes, although there was opposition to his support for the ill-fated White Paper *In Place of Strife*, with its proposals for curbing the power of trade unions. With Labour in Opposition, however, he was faced with a challenge to his support for the EEC.

As a fervent advocate of Britain's membership of the EEC, Taverne was one of the rebel Labour MPs who voted with the

Conservative Government in October 1971. The Lincoln constituency Labour Party, on the other hand, was firmly opposed to Britain's entering the EEC. In June 1971 it passed a resolution calling on all members of the PLP to oppose entry, and a year later it voted for Taverne's retirement at the next election.

The events which led to Taverne's rejection at Lincoln in June 1972 were to repeat themselves in the constituency parties of a number of other social democrat Labour MPs throughout the 1970s. Left-wingers in Lincoln had gradually taken control of the key general management committee, as old loyalists, disillusioned by the performance of Labour Governments, had got fed up and retired. There was also some evidence of a deliberate strategy of infiltration and 'entryism' by groups on the far left. The decision to remove Taverne had been taken by the general management committee without reference to the ordinary members of the party. (A poll, in fact, suggested that they would have liked to see him stay.) Finally, his appeal against the dismissal was turned down by Labour's NEC, which by now was itself beginning to be dominated by the left.

Taverne decided to resign his seat and to fight the consequent by-election as an independent. He hoped that other social democrats in the Labour Party would back him and provoke the split which he now felt sure must come. In December 1972 he had dinner with Roy Jenkins at an Italian restaurant in Uxbridge and asked him to come and speak on his behalf. 'It will finish you in the Labour Party,' he admitted, 'but you could then lead a split away and form a new social democratic party.' Jenkins considered the proposition and speculated that he could probably bring about a dozen MPs with him. However, although he was torn, he did not feel the time was yet right for a breakaway. He did, however, resist pressure to go to Lincoln and speak against Taverne, as both Anthony Crosland and Denis Healey did. Roy Jenkins now wishes that he had backed Taverne and provoked a split in the Labour Party in the early 1970s.

Taverne did not receive much encouragement from other social democrat colleagues in the House of Commons. He recalls being given a lift home by Robert Maclennan, Labour MP for Caithness and Sutherland and a strong pro-Marketeer, on the night before his appeal to the NEC was rejected.

He urged that if I did as I proposed I could never under any circumstances return to the Labour Party; nor would the party ever split. It would surely be better to accept my fate and retire gracefully at the next General Election. I could then make a comeback when, as must surely happen one day, the Labour Party returned to sanity and the quarrels over the Common Market were only a distant memory.[8]

Taverne was undaunted, however, and after forcing a by-election in Lincoln by resigning his seat, he offered himself to the electorate as a Democratic Labour candidate. 'Personally I would have preferred to call myself "Social Democrat",' he wrote shortly afterwards, 'but this is not, or not yet at any rate, a familiar term to most voters.'[9] His campaign was based on the policy issues of support for Britain's membership of the EEC, industrial democracy and a prices and incomes policy, and on the point of principle that MPs were representatives rather than delegates, should stand by commitments on which they were elected and should not be dictated to by the party caucus.

The result of the by-election on 1 March 1973 was a staggering victory for Taverne. He won with a majority of 13,000 over the official Labour candidate, winning 58 per cent of the vote against 23 per cent for Labour and 18 per cent for the Conservatives. It was clear that he had taken a significant number of votes from both the main parties. Among commentators the victory caused a brief flurry of excitement over the possibility of a new alignment in British politics, especially as only three months before the Liberals had won the apparently rock-solid Conservative seat of Sutton and Cheam. In October Taverne himself launched a national Campaign for Social Democracy, which aimed to put up candidates in the next General Election and to 'change the course of British politics'. In a book published early in 1974, *The Future of the Left*, he argued that what had happened in Lincoln was not just an isolated, freakish event, and that there was now a real prospect of the Labour Party's splitting and the formation of a new social democratic party in Britain.

The event which, in the judgement of Taverne and many others, prevented this prospect from being realised was the unexpected Labour victory in the General Election of February

1974. In power for the next five years, the party moved back to broadly social democratic policies once again, accepting the nation's verdict in favour of staying in the EEC, committing itself to the maintenance of the nuclear deterrent, generally forswearing further nationalisation and imposing a tight incomes policy, to the growing perturbation of the unions. Some of its actions – in particular, the trade-offs between Government support for restrictive practices and the closed shop and union support for the tough economic policies – offended leading social democrats, but on the whole they were prepared to turn a blind eye to them. They were more worried, however, by the steady advance of the left, which was angry once again at the apparent betrayal of socialist principles by a Labour Government. There was also growing concern about the failure of the party leadership to halt this advance. The demands made by the International Monetary Fund and the circumstance of a tiny Commons majority might be enough to prevent socialism from reigning supreme in Westminster or Whitehall, but they were hardly sufficient to check the steady progress of the left in the party as a whole.

Just how steady that progress was had already begun to be apparent to a number of right-wing Labour MPs. By the end of 1974 three others had suffered the same fate as Taverne. Eddie Milne had been ousted by his constituency party in Blyth after pursuing a campaign against corruption in the Labour Party in the North-East. Like Taverne, he had subsequently stood as an Independent Labour candidate and had been re-elected. Eddie Griffiths, MP for Sheffield Brightside since 1968, had fallen victim to what he described as 'a well-planned coup led by extremists', and Frank Tomney, a leading Gaitskellite in the 1950s and early 1960s, had been thrown out by his local party at Hammersmith North. Other MPs, including Richard Crawshaw in Liverpool Toxteth, were in trouble with their constituency parties, and one, Edward Lyons in Bradford West, had faced a call for his retirement because of his support for the EEC, but they had managed to beat off the left-wing challenge.

The longest and most highly publicised dispute between a Labour MP and his constituency party was that involving Reg Prentice at Newham North-East. In many ways Prentice was not a typical member of the social democratic group of Labour MPs. An old-time, working-class loyalist, he had not been involved in the Campaign for Democratic Socialism and was not a fervent pro-Marketeer. Indeed, he had voted against the principle of entry in October 1971. However, he had become increasingly worried by, and had spoken out in the party about, the growing influence of the left and the policy of appeasement with respect to the unions. Relations with his local party became increasingly acrimonious, and eventually, in July 1975, the general management committee voted to invite him to retire as MP. Like Taverne, he appealed to the NEC, and his appeal was rejected.

The Prentice affair had several important consequences. It increased the alarm of leading Labour social democrats about the growing influence of the far left and the leadership's apparent reluctance to do anything about it. Roy Jenkins and Shirley Williams had taken up Prentice's case in the higher councils of the party, while Neville Sandelson, the right-wing MP for Hayes and Harlington, who was also in trouble with his constituency party, had tried to whip up support for him among fellow Labour MPs. All three, however, had come up against indifference and a reluctance to become involved. Partly as a result of what had happened at Newham, Reg (later Lord) Underhill, the Labour Party's national agent, was asked to prepare a report on the infiltration of the party by extreme left-wing groups. His report on 'Entryist Activities', which dealt in particular with the activities of a group known as the Militant Tendency, which made no secret of its Marxist views, went to the NEC in November 1975, but it was never published or discussed, much to the annoyance of Sandelson and Tom Bradley.

The events at Newham also played a part in influencing a group of social democratically inclined Labour local councillors to launch a campaign to expose and reverse the growing hold of the far left. The Social Democratic Alliance (SDA), as it became known, was formally launched in June 1975 by a group of Labour Party members who felt that the party was 'being driven from its historic course by an intolerant dogmatism alien to its socialist tradition and democratic system' and wished to make sure that it continued to be a party 'which aims at creating a democratic socialist society and works within the British system of Parliamentary democracy'.[10]

The leading lights behind the founding of the SDA were Douglas Eden and Stephen Haseler, both polytechnic lecturers and Labour members of the Greater London Council. Peter Stephenson, the editor of a small but influential right-wing Labour monthly, *Socialist Commentary*, became the SDA's first chairman, and its foundation was welcomed both by Roy Jenkins and by Reg Prentice, for whose struggle in Newham it declared its unequivocal support.

The SDA never became more than a small pressure group operating on the fringe of the Labour Party. From the beginning it chose to pursue an almost hysterical witch-hunt against the left, which alienated many leading social democrats. Its publications carried personal attacks on individual left-wingers which those who might otherwise have been sympathetic to its aims found difficult to stomach. Stephenson resigned as chairman because of his disquiet about a SDA newsletter published in September 1975 which had accused eleven members of Labour's NEC of having friendly feelings towards East European dictatorships on the basis of their contributions to the Communist newspaper, the *Morning Star*, and to Radio Moscow. Harold Wilson condemned the exercise as McCarthyite, a charge supported by most social democrats in Parliament.

The SDA was not the only group to be set up in the mid-1970s to champion the cause of social democracy in the Labour Party. In December 1974 right-wing MPs followed the practice that had long been adopted by those on the left and set up their own Manifesto Group within the PLP. Early in 1977 a much larger group of social democrats, both inside and outside Parliament, came together to form the Campaign for Labour Victory, in many ways a resurrection of the Campaign for Democratic Socialism of the early 1960s.

The need for a rallying of social democrat MPs had become apparent in the period between the two elections of 1974. Following a long period in which the right had easily dominated the PLP there was a large intake of left-wingers after the February election. The influence of these new recruits was seen in the election of the veteran left-winger Ian Mikardo as chairman of the PLP in March, when the moderate vote was split four ways. MPs on the right of the party realised that they must organise themselves and beat the left-wing Tribune Group at its own game.

The title of the Manifesto Group was significant. It had originally considered calling itself the Social Democratic Group, but that suggestion was ruled out because of the associations with Taverne's campaign. The group was a coalition of old-time loyalists, who felt the Government needed support against increasingly strong attack from the left, and younger intellectuals, who wanted the group to act as a forum for the discussion and reformulation of democratic socialist philosophy. Both elements were agreed on the importance of a Labour Government's sticking to the manifesto on which it had been elected and not being deflected by Conference decisions or pressures from the left into introducing new or contradictory policies. In that respect the group's title was an accurate reflection of what its members stood for.

Although some of the older loyalists, like Michael Stewart, MP for Fulham, Thomas Urwin, MP for Houghton-le-Spring, and James Wellbeloved, MP for Erith and Crayford, assumed active roles in the new group, it was the younger social democrats who took over most of the key positions. The first chairman was Dickson Mabon; the secretary was John Horam, a young economist who had been elected for Gateshead West in 1970; and the treasurer was Neville Sandelson.

Among the most active members of the steering committee were David Marquand and Brian Walden. Two new MPs elected in 1974 were soon to become leading members of the group. They were John Cartwright, MP for Woolwich West, and Ian Wrigglesworth, MP for Teesside, Thornaby, who took over as secretary in 1976, when John Horam replaced Dickson Mabon as chairman.

The Manifesto Group was probably more important as a forum for the working out of a distinctive social democratic philosophy in the Labour Party than for its work as a pressure group in Parliament. In March 1977 it published a document entitled *What We Must Do – A Democratic Socialist Approach to Britain's Crisis*, which rejected both Conservative free-market and Marxist strategies for the future development of the economy and argued that only a democratic socialist approach would bring about the changes required and still preserve individual liberties. The authors included David Marquand, John Horam, John Mackintosh, John Roper and two recently elected MPs, Giles Radice and Bryan Magee. Throughout the late 1970s the group called for the establishment of a permanent incomes policy.

The Campaign for Labour Victory (CLV) was the most broadly based and in many ways the most important of the three campaigning groups set up by social democrats in the Labour Party in the mid-1970s. It developed out of a meeting held at the St Ermin's Hotel, London, organised by Ian Wrigglesworth and John Cartwright and chaired by William Rodgers, in the aftermath of the October 1976 Party Conference at Blackpool. The Conference, at which both the new leader, James Callaghan, and the deputy leader, Denis Healey, were shouted down by the left, was generally considered to have been a disaster for the social democrats. It had passed motions calling for the nationalisation of the big four banks and the seven biggest insurance companies and had endorsed a document produced by the NEC, *Labour's Programme for 1976*, which contained no mention of the North Atlantic Treaty Organisation (NATO) or of an incomes policy but revived Clause Four socialism with a call for the public ownership of the leading companies in every key sector of industry. Elections for the NEC had produced significant left-wing gains, and the continuing leftward drift of local constituency parties was only too apparent from the speeches of the delegates from that section of the floor.

Another left-wing victory at the end of the year alarmed social democrats and encouraged them to rally their forces. This was the confirmation by the NEC of the appointment as the party's national youth officer of Andrew Bevan, a leading supporter of the Militant Tendency and a self-proclaimed Marxist. The decision was a direct snub to James Callaghan, who had asked the NEC not to appoint Bevan, and a victory for Tony Benn, who had argued for his appointment on the grounds that Marxism was 'a legitimate stream of thought' within the British Labour Party.

The CLV was launched at a meeting chaired by William

Rodgers in the Methodist Central Hall, Westminster on 19 February 1977. Its manifesto began: 'The Labour Party must be a broad national party open to all who believe in democratic socialism based on our Parliamentary system' and went on to proclaim that 'socialism must be based on the need for practical policies to secure social justice and equality, and not on narrow ideological class warfare.' It set itself a wide-ranging and ambitious range of objectives: to reverse the decline in party membership, to encourage moderates to go to meetings again, to change the constitution of local Labour parties so that ordinary members had more say, to reform the NEC and the national headquarters at Transport House, and to change the balance of power in the party nationally so that trade unions and constituency activists had less say and rank-and-file members and local councillors more.

It was in the CLV that the social democrats first developed the idea of 'one man, one vote' which was to become for some the sticking-point over staying in the party four years later. One of the first people to see that the right could hope to win back its old influence in the party only by outflanking the left in its demands for greater democracy and accountability in the party was Jim Daly, a former trade union research officer and Greater London councillor, who was now a senior polytechnic lecturer in industrial relations and one of the founder members of the CLV. In an important article in *Socialist Commentary* in October 1976 he had argued that the influx of the professional middle classes into the Labour Party had made it inevitable that MPs would be rendered more accountable and that constituency parties would demand a greater say in policy-making. Social democrats should welcome this development, he said, and should work for a fully democratic Labour Party:

There is an irrefutable case to be made for all the members of the Labour Party to have the automatic right to vote for all the principal officers of the constituency and the National Executive as well as candidates for parliament and local government. . . . A more democratic party will attract more members and be less susceptible to unrepresentative pressure groups and self-promoting cliques.[11]

The driving force behind the CLV came from a group of young men outside Parliament who were in some ways reminiscent of the group which had launched the Campaign for Democratic Socialism seventeen years earlier. The chairman of the new campaign was Clive Wilkinson, the 39-year-old leader of the Labour group on Birmingham City Council. The treasurer was Ben Stoneham, a 29-year-old Cambridge graduate who worked as personal aide to the chairman of the National Coal Board and was Labour candidate in the 1977 Saffron Walden by-election. Alec McGivan, a 23-year-old Oxford graduate, was recruited as full-time organiser. The other key figure in the CLV's organisation was Roger Liddle, 29, another Oxford graduate who was working as personal assistant to Bill Rodgers in the Ministry of Transport.

The founding of the CLV was a sign of the acute anxiety felt by many social democrats by 1977. Some of them were already privately beginning to regard a split from the Labour Party as inevitable. From the outset Alec McGivan felt that the campaign might well be the springboard for the launching of a new party. He was no doubt influenced by his experiences at Oxford, where he had set up a new Democratic Labour Club because the old Labour Club had been taken over so completely by the left. Publicly, however, no mention was made of the possibility of a split, and the organisers of the campaign concentrated on trying to get backing for their programme in the party. They regarded it as particularly important to win the support of leading moderates in the Cabinet. However, only three, Shirley Williams, Bill Rodgers and David Owen, the recently appointed Foreign Secretary, enthusiastically agreed to join the campaign and to appear on CLV platforms. Others, like Denis Healey, Merlyn Rees and Peter Shore, declined to commit themselves publicly to the CLV. Roy Hattersley gave the campaign his guarded support but expressed reservations about backing a sectional group within the party.

There was an added problem, in that several leading social democrats had already left the Labour Party or had distanced themselves from it. The most serious loss was undoubtedly that of Roy Jenkins, throughout the 1964 to 1974 period the effective leader of the social democrats in the Labour Party, whose departure to Brussels as President of the EEC in January 1977 signalled the end of his career in the Labour Party. Before leaving, he had made a last bid to gain the party leadership but had polled only fifty-six votes, a sign of the weakness of the social democrats' hold on the PLP. George Thomson had taken the same route out of the Labour Party four years earlier. Christopher Mayhew, another pro-Marketeer and former Minister, had joined the Liberals in July 1974. Reg Prentice had resigned from the Labour Government at the end of 1976 to sit as an independent MP. David Marquand had resigned his seat to become chief adviser to Roy Jenkins in Brussels. Brian Walden, one of the ablest members of the Manifesto Group, had quit politics in 1977 to become presenter of the London Weekend Television programme *Weekend World*. Finally, sudden death removed two of the brightest Labour social democrats, Anthony Crosland (in 1977) and John Mackintosh (in 1978).

Several of these departures from politics were a sign of disillusionment not just with the Labour Party but also with the prospects for forming a new social democratic party. The omens did not look good. The four candidates put up in the February 1974 General Election by Dick Taverne's Campaign for Social Democracy lost their deposits, polling only between 0.8 and 2.4 per cent of the vote. Taverne himself failed to hold Lincoln in the October election and abandoned his political career. Reg Prentice seriously considered the possibility of standing as a social democrat and appeared on a platform with Taverne in February 1977 calling for the formation of a new party, but by the end of the year he had joined the Conservatives and was dismissing the idea of a new centre party as 'a form of escapism'. His defection to the Tories, which caused bitterness among those who had fought hard to defend him in the Labour Party, lessened the chance of any breakaway by social democrats, as it made it easy for the left to portray them as being on their way to join Mrs Thatcher.

Despite their evident difficulties and doubts, the social democrats left in the Labour Party went through 1977 and 1978 in a moderately optimistic mood. They had high hopes that Callaghan would prove to be tougher on the left than Wilson had been, and that he would act on the Underhill Report to halt infiltration of the constituency parties. The pact with the Liberals from March 1977 to the autumn of 1978 kept nationalisation off the agenda and allowed the Governnment to moderate public spending and to pursue a tight incomes policy. There were also encouraging signs that the unions were moving to the right once again. Terry Duffy's election as President of the engineering workers was seen as a particularly hopeful development.

Admittedly, the 1978 Conference was worrying, with the unions voting against the 5 per cent pay policy and the left consolidating its hold on the NEC. However, Conference rejected a left-wing proposal to change the method of electing the party leader and, in a rather confused vote, apparently accepted a compromise on the issue of the re-selection of MPs by their constituency parties between elections, which waived the process if parties passed a vote of confidence in their sitting Member. (The left had sought compulsory re-selection of all MPs.)

Throughout the early part of 1979 the energies of all in the Labour Party – including, appropriately enough, the supporters of the CLV – were concentrated on the forthcoming General Election. The manifesto on which the party fought represented a considerable triumph for the leadership over the left. A secret draft prepared under the Prime Minister's instructions re-placed the manifesto drafted at Transport House on the basis of the NEC's proposals and *Labour's Programme for 1976*. As a result, proposals for the nationalisation of leading companies, the abolition of the House of Lords and a Freedom of Information Bill were dropped, and Callaghan took the party into the election on a cautious, even conservative, manifesto which contrasted with Mrs Thatcher's radicalism.

The election proved to be a disaster for the party. Labour's share of the vote dropped to 36.9 per cent, its lowest since 1931. Hardly was the result known than the left launched into an attack on the leadership for what it saw as a betrayal over the manifesto and signalled its clear intention of changing the party constitution to take the election of the leader away from the PLP and to give the NEC ultimate control over the manifesto.

Defeat caused the right also to reflect on the state of the party and on whether anything could now be done to save it. In the aftermath of the election two social democrats with very different backgrounds and perspectives put pen to paper. Both came to the same conclusion in their writings: that the Labour

Party in which they had worked and fought was effectively beyond redemption and that the time had now come for the formation of a new social democratic party.

The first contribution came from David Marquand, the leading Jenkinsite, son of a Labour Privy Councillor and now Professor of Contemporary History and Politics at Salford University. In an article in the July 1979 issue of the literary magazine *Encounter* entitled 'Inquest on a Movement', he delivered an eloquent obituary on the traditional Labour Party, which had been brought down, he suggested, as in classical tragedy, by a combination of its own *hubris* and an avenging Fate. Specifically, he accused the party of being taken over by an aggressive proletarianism which discounted the legacy and contribution of middle-class intellectuals. He concluded:

My emotional loyalties are to the Labour Party. I would find it horribly painful to have to accept the notion that it has now outlived its usefulness; and although I can see that the facts point in that direction, I still hope that by some miracle, the party can return to its old vocation as the chief vehicle of radical reform in this country. But the chances do not seem to me good.

I do not believe that the job of revising traditional welfare-state social democracy can be done within the Labour Party or that active Labour politicians can contribute much to it.[12]

The second analysis of what had gone wrong with the Labour Party and what needed to be done to save social democracy came from Stephen Haseler, the co-founder of the SDA, who came from a humbler background than Marquand and whose experience was rooted in local rather than national politics. In his book *The Tragedy of Labour*, published in 1980, he offered a very different explanation for why social democracy had ceased to be the guiding principle of the Labour Party. For Haseler, it was the result of the party's abandonment of populism and its surrender to the middle-class socialist intelligentsia. Yet his conclusion was substantially the same as Marquand's:

Labour's leaders no longer look for inspiration to social democracy. Nor are their guiding principles drawn from the early English utopian, Christian, Owenite tradition. What is left? Put starkly, a British version of the West European communist tradition. . . .

The emergence of a new political force in British politics – whether created by the transformation of one of the major parties, a realignment, the Liberals, or from outside the political elite – will break the cycle of alternating failures.[13]

(*Spectator, 29 March 1981*)

CHAPTER 5

The Birth of the
Social Democratic Party
3 May 1979 to 26 March 1981

The story of the birth of the Social Democratic Party really begins with the General Election of May 1979 and ends with the launch in the Connaught Rooms nearly two years later. It involves the coming together of three different groups: Roy Jenkins in Brussels and his close associates in England, the Social Democratic Alliance and other local Democratic Labour groups around the country; and last and most important, David Owen, Shirley Williams and William Rodgers, or the 'Gang of Three' as they later came to be called, and their supporters at Westminster.

The members of each of these groups had their own different reasons for being dissatisfied with the Labour Party and came independently to the conclusion that they must leave and attempt to set up a new party. Jenkins and his followers were not only the first to champion this cause but also the most fully committed to it and the most enthusiastic about the whole idea of a new centre party in British politics. The SDA also took early steps to distance itself from the Labour Party, although for some time its members went on hoping that they could purge the party of its left-wing element and restore it to what it had been in its Gaitskellite heyday. The 'Gang of Three' and their supporters were the most reluctant to leave the party which they had served for so long. For them the decision to break became irrevocable only after Labour had, as far as they were concerned, abandoned the basic principles of Parliamentary democracy by seeking to make MPs delegates rather than representatives and by taking the election of the leader out of the hands of MPs.

The story of how these three streams, with their very different eddies and currents, finally came to flow together at the beginning of 1981 is a complex and confusing one. Readers may find it helpful to refer to the chronology printed at the beginning of this book. There is at least no doubt about its starting-point, however. The result of the 1979 General Election made a realignment in British politics more likely than it had been at any time since the war. As one of those involved in the formation of the SDP put it:

With a right-wing and unpopular Tory Government in power, Labour bound to move to the left in Opposition, Shirley Williams out of the House of Commons, and Roy Jenkins watching it all from Brussels and waiting to come back, you had a pretty combustible combination.

The SDA was in the most hawkish mood and the quickest off the mark after the election. In June 1979 it changed its structure to become a federation of local social democratic groups around the country, whose members were not necessarily required to be in the Labour Party. This was a response partly to the fact that several of the SDA's most prominent members had by now been expelled from the party for their attacks on the left and also partly to the emergence of independent democratic Labour groups in various places. The largest of these, with around 200 members, had been set up in Scunthorpe by Cyril Nottingham, a former leader of the Labour group on the borough council, who had been expelled from the party after providing evidence for the Underhill Report on left-wing infiltration. Within a year the SDA claimed forty such local groups with a total of about 2000 members.

The Jenkinsites were also stirring soon after the election. Throughout his time in Brussels Roy Jenkins had kept in close touch with many of his old supporters in the Labour Party, particularly Matthew Oakeshott, a young Oxford graduate who had been his political adviser at the Home Office, and David Marquand, who had returned to an academic post in England after working for a year as his chief adviser. Marquand sent Jenkins a copy of his *Encounter* article in July and had dinner with him shortly afterwards in Strasbourg, during the first session of the new directly elected European Parliament. He recalls:

Roy was speculating in a vague way about what he would do when he came back from Brussels in eighteen months' time. We talked about the possibilities of forming a new party and mentioned the names of Bill Rodgers, David Owen and Shirley Williams.

Other former Jenkinsites were having similar thoughts. At a lunch of the National Committee for Electoral Reform shortly after the election Marquand met Colin Phipps, a petroleum geologist who had been Labour MP for Dudley West from 1974 to 1979. Phipps had become convinced that the Labour Party was beyond redemption when the NEC had ruled that those, like him, who wanted to stand in the European elections would have to give up their Westminster seats first. By the summer of 1979 he had become a convinced believer in a new breakaway social democratic party. The election had also reawakened similar thoughts in the mind of Dick Taverne.

However convinced they themselves might be of the desirability of setting up a new party, the Jenkinsites were generally agreed on the importance of involving Shirley Williams, Bill Rodgers or David Owen in the venture if possible. If one or more of them were at the helm with Roy Jenkins, the new vessel that they were planning to launch would stand a much better chance of staying afloat. They did not have high hopes of luring all three aboard. Rodgers, who was closest to Jenkins, seemed the most likely; Shirley Williams, who was emotionally the most strongly tied to the Labour Party and also the most indecisive, seemed a possible but uncertain ally; while Owen, who as Foreign Secretary had not enjoyed good relations with Jenkins, was regarded as the least likely recruit.

At this stage the mood of the 'Gang of Three' was one of wait-and-see. None of them was in any hurry to leave the party to which they had all belonged for so long and which they were still actively serving. Both Rodgers and Owen had important Shadow Cabinet posts in the areas of defence and energy, while Shirley Williams, although out of Parliament and with no immediate desire to return, was still on Labour's NEC. All three pinned their hopes on the possibility that Jim Callaghan might prove another Gaitskell and save the party from sliding irrevocably to the left.

These hopes were somewhat dimmed by the results of the Labour Party Conference at Brighton in October, which voted both for the mandatory re-selection of MPs and for the vesting of control over the manifesto in the NEC. Admittedly, there was room for a change of mind over these issues since, as constitutional changes, they had to come up for ratification the following year. The left won another significant victory in securing dominant representation on the Commission of Inquiry which the Conference set up to investigate the party's finances and membership and to make recommendations about a new way of electing the leader. Callaghan's speech at the end of the Conference was, by general consent, a lack-lustre performance, which suggested to many on the right that he did not have the stomach for a fight.

The immediate effect of the Conference on the 'Gang of Three' and their supporters, however, was to fortify them in their resolve to try to save the Labour Party from within. Working as a team, with Bill Rodgers and David Owen operating in the Shadow Cabinet and all three at CLV meetings, they tried first to secure representation for the PLP on the Commission of Inquiry and then to persuade the unions to reverse their votes on the constitutional changes. In the first object they succeeded; in the second they were only narrowly to fail.

Meanwhile, the whole issue of the formation of a new centre party in Britain was suddenly thrown into the public domain by the Dimbleby Lecture which Roy Jenkins delivered on BBC television at the end of November under the title 'Home Thoughts from Abroad'. Jenkins called for a strengthening of what he described as the 'radical centre' to break the constricting rigidity of the party system. Although he did not actually say that he intended to launch a new party on his return from Brussels, that was the clear impression that the lecture gave to many of his friends and supporters. On the evening that it was broadcast Jenkins and his wife dined with Bill Rodgers, Dick Taverne, David Marquand, Ian Wrigglesworth and their wives and discussed the feasibility of launching a new social democratic party.

Just over a week after the Dimbleby Lecture, on 30 November, Bill Rodgers made a speech at Abertillery, in South Wales, in which he gave the Labour Party a year to save itself. The speech, which was curiously under-reported in the press yet brought Rodgers his biggest ever postbag to date, was the first public statement by one of the 'Gang of Three' to impose a

'I came . . . . I saw . . . . I thought about it.'

(Daily Telegraph, 16 January 1981)

deadline on Labour's sorting itself out. Rodgers said that if the left wanted a fight to the finish, it could have one and hinted that if the left won, he and others would leave the party. On his way back to London he stopped off at Roy Jenkins's country house at East Hendred, near Wantage in South Oxfordshire. Shirley Williams was also there. Together the three of them discussed what Rodgers described as 'the state of the nation'.

The Dimbleby Lecture galvanized several other social democrats into action. Jim Daly and Clive Lindley, a former Labour Parliamentary candidate who ran a very successful motorway catering business, rang up Roy Jenkins in Brussels to offer him their services. They set up a small research organisation, rather grandly titled the Radical Centre for Democratic Studies in Industry and Society, which, operating from the front room of Daly's west London home, produced for Jenkins a press cutting and information service on the political scene in Britain.

The lecture also inspired Colin Phipps to gather a group of former Jenkinsites in Parliament and others interested in the launching of a new party. They included Dick Taverne, David Marquand, Clive Lindley, Jim Daly, Lord Harris of Greenwich, Stephen Haseler of the SDA, Michael Barnes, Labour MP for Brentford and Chiswick from 1966 to 1974, and John Morgan, the broadcaster. The group first met on 20 December, when they dined with Roy Jenkins at Brooks's Club. Thereafter they met regularly in London and once in East Hendred. One sitting Labour MP, John Horam, occasionally joined them. Robert Maclennan, the only other MP to be approached to join the group, declined their invitation.

It was not long before a clear division of opinion about the best tactics to adopt showed itself in the group. Broadly, one element, led by Barnes and Phipps, was in favour of proceeding quickly and launching the new party as soon as possible on the strength of the local groups that were already being formed, while the other, led by Marquand and Lindley, urged a more cautious approach and set much greater store by the role of the 'Gang of Three' and others at Westminster. The 'fast movers' showed their impatience with the others and their own conviction that building up local groups was more important than waiting for a break at Westminster. Phipps formed one such group in the West Midlands in the spring of 1980 and Barnes in west London in September. They were also instrumental in forming an Association of Democratic Groups, which parallelled the SDA. The 'slow movers', by contrast, were prepared to bide their time and wait for the pressure of events in the Labour Party to force the 'Gang of Three' and others to break away. By the summer of 1980 the division had become so wide that the group broke up.

Events were to prove the 'slow movers' right. Within a matter of months the 'Gang of Three' and a group of Labour back-benchers were to become committed to forming a new party. They were driven into this position by a sequence of spectacular victories for the left which began at the Labour Party's special conference in Wembley on 31 May 1980 and ended at a similar gathering in the same place eight months later.

A conference held by the CLV in Birmingham shortly before the first special conference shows both how near to and how far from contemplating a break with the Labour Party the 'Gang of Three' were. Morale in the CLV as a whole was by now low. In the words of Alec McGivan, 'We were trying to rally the troops, but somehow the troops just weren't there.' There was disappointment at Callaghan's failure to give a lead and at equivocation on the part of prominent figures on the centre-right of the party, like Denis Healey, Roy Hattersley and Merlyn Rees.

At this conference Jim Daly, Clive Lindley and others clearly indicated their intention of leaving the party sooner or later. Both Shirley Williams and Bill Rodgers made hawkish speeches suggesting that the fight within the party could not go on for ever and that there must be a definite time limit. Owen, however, said that social democrats must stay in and fight even if it took ten or twenty years to win the battle. At the end of the conference he indicated privately that if the CLV was going to be a vehicle for launching a new party, he wanted nothing to do with it. A few days after the conference Shirley Williams told a meeting of the Manifesto Group that she regarded the idea of forming a new social democratic party as 'all nonsense'. She said, 'I am not interested in a third party. I do not believe it has a future.'[1]

The Wembley special conference was a grim experience for

those social democrats who attended it. In fact, many did not bother to go, regarding the whole occasion as an expensive and unnecessary jamboree for the left, to which it had been a serious mistake for the leadership to agree. The policy document which the conference endorsed, *Peace, Jobs, Freedom*, was strongly anti-EEC and pro-unilateralist and envisaged an economic policy which depended more on import controls than on incomes policy. Inside the conference hall Owen was booed and hissed when he tried to defend multilateralism, an experience which many consider decisive in changing his mind about staying in the Labour Party. Outside the hall, at a lunch-time fringe meeting, Tony Benn launched a new left-wing umbrella group, the Rank and File Mobilising Committee, to co-ordinate the campaign for the mandatory re-selection of MPs, wider control over the manifesto and a new system for electing the party leader.

The conference provoked an outraged response from several social democrats. Tom Ellis, the pro-Common Market MP for Wrexham, denounced the section of the new policy document on the EEC as 'unadulterated hypocrisy'. Neville Sandelson issued a similarly condemnatory statement. The SDA said that Callaghan's acceptance of *Peace, Jobs, Freedom* represented 'the final sell-out of the moderate and democratic traditions of the Labour Party by a bankrupt leadership'. In Bill Rodgers Wembley produced a mood of grim defiance and strengthened his resolve to fight on. I remember meeting him as he was pacing the bare, glass-walled corridors that circle the conference hall. 'The left are better organised than I have ever known them,' he said. 'What we need is a war book of what can and should be done week by week and month by month.'

Close observers are agreed that it was on Owen that the May special conference had the greatest effect. At a CLV reception on the terrace of the House of Commons in June he was very much more friendly towards those who were talking about splitting from the party than he had been a few weeks earlier. His exasperation with the Labour Party had further increased when John Silkin, a fellow member of the Shadow Cabinet, gave notice to a meeting of the Labour Common Market Safeguards Committee of a motion to be put to the next party Conference committing a Labour Government to withdrawing

Britain from the EEC. Silkin's action, which had been taken without consultation with his Shadow Cabinet colleagues, prompted Owen to suggest to Shirley Williams and Bill Rodgers that they should issue a joint statement saying that they would leave the Labour Party if it adopted withdrawal as official party policy. The others were initially rather reluctant to adopt this course, but they agreed, and the statement, the first public declaration by the 'Gang of Three', was issued on 7 June.

Yet although they had now issued a threat to leave the Labour Party, none of the three was yet finally committed, either in his or her own mind or publicly, to the inevitability of a break. On 8 June Shirley Williams again made clear her distaste for a new centre party, which she dismissed as having 'no roots, no principles, no philosophy and no values'. None of the three responded publicly to an address which Roy Jenkins gave to the Parliamentary Press Gallery the following day, when he repeated his call for a realignment of the 'radical centre'. It was another eloquent performance. Jenkins described the present state of British politics as 'two and a half bottles, one labelled Conservatives, the next Labour, the third Liberal' and compared the new party with an experimental aeroplane which might either 'soar in the sky' or equally well 'finish up a few fields from the end of the runway'.

Meanwhile, within the Labour Party things were continuing to go the left's way. On 15 June, after a weekend meeting at Bishop's Stortford in Hertfordshire, the Commission of Inquiry endorsed the principle of mandatory re-selection of MPs and came out in favour of an electoral college to elect the party leader. Owen and Rodgers, together with other centre-right members of the Shadow Cabinet, were furious at what they regarded as Callaghan's sell-out to the left. They saw the electoral college as a device which would prevent the leader from being accountable primarily to Members of Parliament and would put him instead at the beck and call of left-wing constituency and union activists. Rodgers denounced it on the BBC *World At One* programme as an unacceptable constitutional innovation. He was also angry about a Labour Party political broadcast on defence the previous week, over which he, the front-bench defence spokesman, had not been consulted and which had taken a strongly unilateralist line. In a statement issued after Wembley, Neville Sandelson had said that it might be necessary for Labour supporters to vote for another party at the next election to ensure that the 'authoritarian minority' now in control of the party did not come to power.

July brought no better news for the social democrats. The list of resolutions submitted for the Party Conference to be held at the end of September made it inevitable that calls for unilateral disarmament, withdrawal from the EEC and re-nationalisation without compensation of industries de-nationalised by the Conservative Government would be high on the agenda and likely to command majority support. The NEC made clear its intention of moving from the platform a resolution in favour of the establishment of an electoral college to elect the party leader and also expressed its support for measures which would give local Labour parties much more control over Labour councillors.

It was in response to this situation that the 'Gang of Three', at Bill Rodgers's suggestion, decided to write an open letter to their fellow members of the Labour Party. The letter, which went through several drafts, was published in the *Guardian* on 1 August. It castigated the Labour Party for pursuing policies 'based on bureaucratic centralism and state control, policies that offer no improvement in the quality of life'. It accused the NEC of flirting with 'extremists who regard democracy as a sham' and predicted that acceptance of the changes being sought in the party's constitution and method of electing its leader would end representative democracy as it was commonly practised and understood in Britain.

The penultimate paragraph of the open letter dealt with the all-important question of whether the 'Gang of Three' would remain to fight in the party or forsake it to form a new one. It was largely the work of Shirley Williams and, by a careful choice of words, managed to reconcile her oft-repeated repudiation of the idea of a new centre party with her growing feeling that a breakaway from Labour might have to come:

If the NEC remains committed to pursuing its present course and if, consequently, fears multiply among the people, then support for a Centre Party will strengthen as disaffected voters move away from Labour. We have already said that we will not support a Centre Party for it would lack roots and a coherent philosophy. But if the Labour Party abandons its democratic and internationalist principles, the argument may grow for a new democratic socialist party to establish itself as a party of conscience and reform committed to those principles. We are not prepared to abandon Britain to divisive and even cruel Tory policies because electors do not have an opportunity to vote for an acceptable Socialist alternative to a Conservative Government.

This open letter marked an important stage in the gestation of the SDP. It opened the door to a breakaway while admitting the possibility that the Labour Party might still be saved for social democracy. Although they had issued their threat to leave the 'Gang of Three' still hoped that they might never have to carry it out.

The remarks and behaviour of the 'Gang' during the summer continued to indicate a similar degree of equivocation. For example, Bill Rodgers gave a strong hint that he was contemplating a breakaway when he said in an interview on the Tyne-Tees Television programme *Face the Press* on 3 August that if the Labour Party failed to appeal to large numbers of democratic socialists, 'then the argument will grow for a new democratic socialist party'. However, no one was working harder than he was to persuade his colleages in the Shadow Cabinet and key union leaders to accept a 'one man, one vote' formula for the election of the leader, a device with which the 'Gang' still hoped they might be able to beat the left at the party Conference.

Meanwhile others were becoming more impatient and moving rather faster. Predictably, the SDA set the pace. It had moved further and further away from the Labour Party during the first half of 1980, both Douglas Eden, its secretary, and Stephen Haseler, its chairman, having been expelled from their local Labour parties. On 24 July the SDA announced that it would be running up to 200 candidates against official Labour Party nominees in the next General Election if the party committed itself to unilateralism and to the proposed constitutional changes at its autumn Conference. It published a priority list of twenty-seven left-wing MPs to be opposed and an initial list of sixteen candidates, among whom eight were former Labour candidates and ten were still members of the party. In an accompanying statement the SDA declared that 'further efforts to fight back within the confines of a Labour Party controlled by the extremists would be useless.'

Although the SDA's initiative attracted much interest in the press, it gained little support among other Labour social democrats. There was widespread scepticism about the Alliance's ability to field more than a handful of candidates at an election, and even the newly formed Association of Democratic Groups kept its distance. The only MP to give any public approbation to the SDA's move was, predictability, Neville Sandelson, who said that it might well lead to 'a new party formation which in due course would change the face of British politics'.[2]

The Jenkinsites were meanwhile pursuing a rather different tack. They were engaged in informal talks with the Liberals. Over the summer Jenkins himself had several meetings with the Liberal leader, David Steel; Clive Lindley got together with Roger Pincham, chairman of the Liberal Party and candidate for Leominster (where he had been Labour candidate); and David Marquand talked to Liberals in the North-West. Their motives were mixed. Jenkins himself was both temperamentally and ideologically attracted to Liberalism. Indeed, in many ways he was more of a Liberal and Steel more of a Social Democrat. His scheme for a realignment of British politics envisaged a key role for the Liberals in the new radical centre party. There was also a feeling among Jenkins and his supporters that if the worst came to the worst and none of the 'Gang of Three' showed any signs of breaking away from the Labour Party, joining the Liberals might prove a more sensible course than trying to go it alone and forming a new party. That expedient was always seen as a second-best option and was never seriously considered, although there were occasional moments during the summer of 1980 when some Jenkinsites began to fear that the 'Gang' would never make the final break from Labour.

In fact, David Steel played an important role in encouraging Roy Jenkins to wait for the 'Gang of Three' to break with the Labour Party and not to pre-empt them by joining the Liberals or by striking off on his own before the New Year. Steel made it clear that he thought the chances of busting the two-party system would be much better if it was challenged by strong, separate Liberal and social democratic parties than if a few people moved over from Labour to join the Liberals. Indeed, he actively discouraged one Labour MP who actually came to him wanting to join the Liberals, telling him that he thought it better to wait until there was a bigger breakaway from the Labour party.

Publicly, Steel called on the 'Gang of Three' to leave the Labour Party and to start talks with him. Their response was unenthusiastic, however. Bill Rodgers, who, according to friends, had not been impressed by Steel's negotiating abilities during the period of the Lib.–Lab. pact, replied to his invitation, 'We do not support the idea of a centre party, and that includes the Liberals: we are Democratic Socialists seeking to save the Labour Party.' But Steel persisted in believing that the 'Gang of Three' would, in fact, break away and continued to talk to the Jenkinsites. At the Liberal Assembly in September, where David Marquand was the star speaker at a packed fringe meeting, Steel succeeded in carrying the party with him as he recommended working for a close alliance with the new social democratic party which he felt was now almost certain to be established.

Among the leading social democrats in the PLP the accent, in public at least, was still very much on staying on and reforming the party from within rather than quitting. On 22 September, just a week before the start of the party Conference, a group of twelve MPs led by Michael Thomas, the ebullient MP for Newcastle-on-Tyne East, published a statement in *The Times* calling for major but rather vague reforms in the structure of the party. These included measures to allow every member to vote for parliamentary candidates, to change the composition of the NEC, to alter the relationship between trade unions and the party and to devise a new system for electing the leader (but not an electoral college). The other MPs involved in this call included some familiar names – John Roper, John Horam, John Cartwright, Tom Ellis and Ian Wrigglesworth, together with two prominent Scottish back-benchers, George Robertson and Willie Hamilton (best-known as the scourge of the British monarchy), and four old-time moderate loyalists, Thomas Urwin, Eric Ogden, Arthur Palmer and Alan Fitch.

The 'Gang of Three' approached the party Conference in a

gloomy mood. Shirley Williams was, according to her friends, nervous, vacillating and uncertain, one moment protesting her loyalty to the party in which she had grown up and the next moment talking of leaving it. Bill Rodgers and David Owen were cooler and more certain in their own minds. Their decision about their future course would depend entirely on what happened at the Conference. All three were extremely depressed by what they saw as the Shadow Cabinet's lack of will to fight the left's proposals for changes in the party's constitution. As Shirley Williams put it:

It was becoming increasingly clear that Roy Hattersley and Denis Healey and Peter Shore and the others weren't going to join us. The so-called moderates just wouldn't come out of their corners. Their great cry was 'I think I'll just keep my head down.' When your allies won't come out and fight, that really takes the heart out of you.

For several social democrats the proposed constitutional changes were the sticking-point. They were reconciled to the fact that the policy decisions which would be taken at the Conference were going to be 'bad'. On the eve of the Conference Shirley Williams and Tom Bradley, the other leading social democrat on the NEC, let it be known that they would not be speaking from the platform because of their profound disagreements with the NEC over policy. Even if the conference were to vote in favour of unilateral nuclear disarmament and withdrawal from the EEC without a referendum, as it did, the 'Gang of Three' and others had decided that they would still stay in the Labour Party and fight to reverse those decisions, just as social democrats had done after the unilateralist vote at the Scarborough Conference exactly twenty years earlier. If, however, it also voted in favour of the mandatory re-selection of MPs and for an electoral college to elect the leader, many had already decided that they would quit.

In the event, the Conference went worse than anyone had expected. Most of the week was taken up with bitter in-fighting rather than with attacking the Conservative Government. Two MPs, Andrew Faulds on the right and Martin Flannery on the left, had their speeches cut short by the chairman when they started to make personal attacks on other comrades. Conference endorsed the mandatory re-selection of MPs and voted to change the methods of electing the leader but failed to agree on a suitable form of electoral college. It broke up with this central issue still unresolved and with the prospect of another special conference early in the new year to sort it out.

On the evening of the inconclusive Conference vote over the electoral college a group of centre-right MPs met in Shirley Williams's hotel room in Blackpool. Their mood was overwhelmingly one of despair; it was now too late for the Labour Party to save itself. For the first time several talked seriously about breaking away. What had formerly been a matter of principle now became primarily a matter of timing.

Whatever their private feelings now were about the inevitability of a split, publicly at least, the 'Gang of Three' battled on within the Labour Party and refused to concede defeat. They decided to put all their efforts into trying to secure a victory for the 'one man, one vote' principle at the special conference to decide on a method of electing the leader. At a CLV meeting in London on 25 October, they made it clear that they did not regard that principle as negotiable. If they failed to carry it, that would be the end of the road. Significantly, more than a third of those who spoke from the floor at the meeting talked about leaving the Labour Party.

It soon became evident that they were not going to succeed. They had pinned their hopes on the Shadow Cabinet's abandoning its previous fudges and vacillation. In David Owen's words:

We could have recovered if Denis Healey, Roy Hattersley, Merlyn Rees, Eric Varley and John Smith had said we should go to the Conference on 'one man, one vote'. When they ditched that last November inside the Shadow Cabinet I knew they had no stomach for a proper fight. . . . That was the time I knew we had to fight for one member, one vote in January, and if we went down in that conference, then either we created a new party or I would leave politics.[3]

Another event in November confirmed the 'Gang of Three' in their feeling that they were right to be thinking about leaving the party. The election of the veteran left-winger Michael Foot as Labour leader made the prospect of a breakaway much easier to contemplate. Had the leadership gone to Foot's major challenger, Denis Healey, most social democrats would have felt duty-bound to give him a chance, perhaps a year, to pull the party round. They had equivocal feelings about the contest. Publicly, they urged Healey to adopt a tougher line towards the left and were disappointed at what they took to be his readiness to compromise. Privately, many of them hoped that he would not win and were secretly relieved by the outcome of the election which provided them with a clear reason for leaving the party.

After Foot's election there was a suggestion in the social democrat camp that Bill Rodgers should stand for the deputy leadership, largely to test the water for a possible breakaway and to establish how many MPs would be likely to follow him. The idea was abandoned, but Rodgers did decide to stand for election to the Shadow Cabinet. After being elected, he withdrew from all discussions about the formation of a new party and involved himself instead in an acrimonious row with Michael Foot about which Shadow portfolio he should be given.

The other members of the 'Gang', by contrast, were now clearly embarking on the process of disengagement from the Labour Party. Owen, who was the most certain in his own mind and the most determined to leave, was already holding almost daily meetings, in his room in the Norman Shaw building just across the road from the House of Commons, with MPs who might be possible recruits to a new party. On 21 November he announced that he would not be seeking re-election to the Shadow Cabinet, a clear indication to his friends that his days in the Labour Party were numbered. A week later Shirley Williams told her former constituency party in Hertford and Stevenage that she could not be a Labour candidate because she could not defend the policies agreed at the party Conference. She said, 'There is no other party in Britain today I would contemplate joining. . . . Britain needs a party of liberty, equality, comradeship, common sense and internationalism.'[4]

On 10 December an important meeting took place at Shirley Williams's flat in Victoria. It was attended by Bill Rodgers,

John Horam, John Roper, Mike Thomas, Ian Wrigglesworth, Robert Maclennan, Matthew Oakeshott and two of Britain's leading academic psephologists, Professor Ivor Crewe and Professor Anthony King, both of Essex University. The message of the two professors to the assembled politicians was that a new social democratic party would have significant electoral support.

Meanwhile the momentum for a new breakaway party was also increasing in other quarters. The SDA, which had finally been proscribed by the Labour Party at the beginning of December, was now firmly committed to building up a new party from the grass roots. Roy Jenkins, contemplating his return to Britain at the beginning of January, felt confident enough, after the Blackpool Conference and the election of Michael Foot, to go it alone if necessary and set up a new centre party. He still hoped, and was increasingly confident, that the 'Gang of Three' would join him, but his supporters had now formed the view that even if they did not, he should go ahead. Soundings among MPs had revealed at least four who would come with him – Tom Bradley, Tom Ellis, Neville Sandelson and Robert Maclennan.

Viewing the prospects of a breakaway from the rather different perspective of Westminster, David Owen was equally determined to go it alone if necessary, and equally certain that he could take with him a group of Labour MPs led by John Horam and Mike Thomas. One of the most delicate and important stages in the gestation of the SDP was the reconciliation of Owen and Jenkins at the end of 1980 and their acknowledgement that they must work together rather than separately if the new party which they were both bent on forming were to have any real chance of success. In the past, as we have already noted, relations between them had not been good and, according to friends, Owen had made it clear that he would have nothing to do with any new party led by Jenkins. He felt that the centre party envisaged in the Dimbleby Lecture did not have much in common with the radical socialist party which he wanted to create. However, at what Jenkins describes as 'an important lunch' at East Hendred at the end of November the two men met to talk over their ideas. Thereafter, whatever their private reservations, they worked together rather than independently to create a new party.

A memorandum written by Owen early in December and subsequently leaked to the press after it had been stolen from his room in the House of Commons, gives an interesting insight into his state of mind at this stage and also into his feelings about Jenkins. It was drawn up after the confrontation between Michael Foot and Bill Rodgers over the latter's Shadow Cabinet post and was designed to provide a clear strategy for those social democrats who were now committed to a break. Much of it was devoted to a discussion about whether it was better to make a clean break from Labour immediately after the special conference early in the new year or to go for a more gradual breakaway, which would culminate in the formation of a new party in October 1981.

On the question of the future leadership of the social democrats, the document said:

Some of our closest allies see Roy still as our potential leader. Others count him as a friend but do not see him as the political leader in the 1980s but as contributing powerfully to the campaign for social democracy. Others see him as a liability, linked to the Liberal–centre party concept and not a social democrat.

The maximum unity can only be achieved if it is accepted that any social democratic organisation will be based on one member, one vote, and that therefore the membership will determine the roles of individuals, but that before such decisions there should be a collective leadership.

The problem with leaving this leadership issue blurred is threefold. Firstly, Roy has in the past been accepted as our leader and for four and a half years was actually voted for as our leader; a natural tendency if the issue is not resolved will be for him to emerge as our leader.

Secondly, Roy is older, therefore letting him emerge as the leader now satisfies the ambitions of those younger by leaving the issue open. Thirdly, the media will want a leader – particularly if we widen it out from the Gang of Three which has been accepted as a collective leadership.

In terms of immediate tactics, Owen's memorandum proposed that the social democrats should organise themselves as a kind of right-wing Militant Tendency within the Labour Party. Those in the Shadow Cabinet and on the NEC should remain in their posts during the run-up to the formation of a new party. The CLV should be ended, and care should be taken not to offend the SDA. Meanwhile, everything should be done to 'escalate the significance' of the coming special conference.

The memorandum reveals Owen's clear conviction that with the acceptance of an electoral college to elect its leader, the Labour Party was beyond redemption. Short of the equivalent of a Bad Godesberg conference during the 1980s, which he indicated that he regarded as an unlikely possibility, the prospect facing Britain was 'to have, after twenty-five years, a further ten years of bad government'. The unacceptability of that prospect, he suggested, 'outweighs the real danger that splitting the left could allow the right a sustained period of government, longer than the thirteen years between 1951 and 1964. The question then becomes how to split.'[5]

By the end of December the 'Gang of Four', as they had now become, were at various stages along the road that would take them out of the Labour Party. Roy Jenkins had travelled the furthest. At a meeting at Clive Lindley's flat on 30 December with his closest supporters, including Matthew Oakeshott, David Marquand and Jim Daly, he decided that he would launch his new party at the end of March, whatever happened. David Owen, although almost equally determined to go, was still engaged in discussions about mounting a last-ditch fight in the party. Bill Rodgers was moving more slowly. Over lunch with Jenkins at East Hendred on 28 December he had said that the earliest he would leave the Labour Party would be after the party Conference in October 1981. Shirley Williams was still very uncertain about going.

Yet within a month the 'Gang of Four' were sufficiently in step to issue the Limehouse Declaration and to set up the Council for Social Democracy as a prelude to forming the new party. This degree of unity was achieved largely through a series of meetings which took place during January at their various homes. The first, which lasted for five hours, was at Jenkins's house at East Hendred on 11 January, just five days after he had finally returned to Britain on relinquishing the Presidency of the EEC. Only Owen and Williams were there. Bill Rodgers was in bed with a bad back, reading Bernard Crick's biography of George Orwell and coming rapidly to the conclusion that he should make the break with the Labour Party sooner rather than later.

The second meeting, and in many ways the most important of all, took place in Shirley Williams's flat on the evening of 14 January. This time all four of the 'Gang' were present. It was, in fact, the first time that they had all met together since the whole idea of forming a new social democratic party had been mooted. At the meeting they discussed the idea that they should make some definite move immediately after the special

'It's a naive domestic Burgundy without any breeding, but I think you'll be amused by its presumption.'
(Sunday Telegraph, 1 February 1981)

conference, which was due to be held in Wembley in ten days' time and which seemed certain to set up an electoral college. They considered a proposal by Shirley Williams that their first step should be to create a Council for Social Democracy as a kind of half-way house which would still keep them in the Labour Party. Roy Jenkins made it clear that he would go along with the idea of such a council only if it was clearly understood that it was a prelude to the setting up of a new party. He was reassured on that point, and the four agreed to meet again the following Sunday, 18 January, to draw up a joint statement to be issued after the Wembley Conference. They also agreed that each of them would bring a representative to that meeting.

The four people chosen as representatives had already been

closely involved in the discussions about forming a new party. Jenkins chose Matthew Oakeshott, his former political adviser at the Home Office, who had been in touch with several MPs in the weeks before Christmas in the hope of persuading them to join a new Jenkinsite party. The obvious choice for Bill Rodgers was Roger Liddle, his former political adviser, who had kept in close touch with him and had been a key figure in the CLV. Alec McGivan, the CLV's secretary, agreed to be David Owen's representative, and Shirley Williams chose John Lyttle, who had been her political adviser when she was Secretary of State for Education.

Meanwhile, several social democrat MPs were beginning to talk openly about making a break with the Labour party. The Liberals' ten-point plan for economic recovery, unveiled by David Steel on 12 January, was publicly welcomed by Neville Sandelson, Tom Ellis, John Horam and Ian Wrigglesworth. Speaking on The Independent Television News programme *News At One* on 15 January, Wrigglesworth admitted that members of the Manifesto Group had discussed leaving the Labour Party but were divided about whether to stay in and fight or to make a break. He went on: 'There are some of us who feel that everything we could possibly do has been done and that it has failed.' Both Owen and the Jenkinsites were still assiduously wooing a number of MPs and keeping them informed of the discussions between the 'Gang'.

The meeting on 18 January was nearly a disaster. It had been fixed to take place at East Hendred but was switched at the last minute to Bill Rodgers's house in Kentish Town, partly because his back was still causing him considerable pain and also because details of the meeting had been leaked in that morning's *Observer*. Shirley Williams, who was in a highly nervous state and furious about the leak, initially refused to come and was only persuaded after a good deal of coaxing from Roy Jenkins. When she arrived, according to one of those present, she treated the assembled company to a 'Harold Wilson-style dressing-down about not talking to the press'. Eventually, however, tempers were calmed and the meeting got down to business. The idea of a Council for Social Democracy was discussed again. Jenkins and Owen stressed that they saw it purely as an interim device and Shirley Williams defended it on the grounds that it would give MPs a breathing space and time in which to sound out their constituency parties. On the question of when the new party should be launched there was a clear difference of opinion. Owen and Jenkins wanted it to be within two months but the other two said that they still wanted to be in the Labour Party after Wembley and were reluctant to contemplate a breakaway until the end of May at the earliest. However, there was agreement that the 'Gang' should issue a joint statement immediately following the Wembley conference, assuming, as seemed inevitable, that it agreed to an electoral college.

During the days leading up to the special conference the members of the 'Gang', and Shirley Williams in particular, came under heavy pressure from senior Labour colleagues, who attempted to persuade them to stay in the party. But although Michael Foot was lavish with his promise of Shadow Cabinet posts, he could not concede the constitutional principle that was their sticking-point. They were now adamant that nothing less than a vote for 'one man, one vote' in the election of the leader would keep them in the party, and without the support of the Shadow Cabinet, there was no possibility of that. Any proposal for an electoral college which did not require the trade unions and local Labour parties to ballot their members was unacceptable.

In the event, the outcome of the special conference on 24 January was worse than the social democrats had feared. The electoral college favoured by Michael Foot and the NEC, which would give the majority say to members of the PLP, was rejected in favour of one in which trade unions would have the biggest vote (40 per cent), with Labour MPs and constituency parties each getting 30 per cent. Paradoxically, for the 'Gang' and their supporters the result proved an unexpected bonus. They could now leave the Labour Party on the popular issue of opposition to the power of the union block vote and not on the unpopular issue of support for Britain's continued membership of the EEC.

On the morning after the Wembley conference the 'Gang' and their four advisers met at David Owen's house in the old docklands area of Limehouse, East London. They were due to be there at 11.30. For once Shirley Williams was early and Bill

Rodgers late. They worked on a statement that had been drafted by Roy Jenkins which was to be released to the press later in the day. After some debate, Jenkins succeded in preserving the sentence with which he had ended the statement, which effectively committed its signatories to forming a new party. It said: 'We believe that the need for a realignment of British politics must now be faced.' The Limehouse Declaration, as it came to be known, was finished at about 1.30 p.m. and was typed by David Owen's American wife, Debbie. The press were summoned for 4 p.m. Alec McGivan went off to photostat the Declaration, and Matthew Oakeshott went to Shirley Williams's flat to get her a suit to wear for the inevitable press photographs.

During the afternoon the 'Gang' were joined at Limehouse by Robert Maclennan, Ian Wrigglesworth, John Roper and Mike Thomas. The press duly arrived, and the 'Gang' posed for photographs on a small canal bridge nearby, Shirley now suitably attired in her Sunday suit and Bill still in his Marks and Spencer pullover. The Limehouse Declaration was issued, and the Council for Social Democracy was launched. Nobody guessed how quickly it would be transformed into a new party.

The following day, after a meeting in David Owen's room, nine Labour MPs announced that they were joining the Council. They were Mike Thomas, Tom Ellis, Ian Wrigglesworth, John Roper, Robert Maclennan, Richard Crawshaw, Neville Sandelson, Tom Bradley and John Horam. Interviewed on the Jimmy Young radio programme, Owen said that the birth of a social democratic party was now 'very close'. David Steel welcomed the Limehouse Declaration, although other Liberals were rather less enthusiastic. Cyril Smith, the colourful and portly MP for Rochdale and an opponent of the Lib.–Lab. pact, said that Liberals should make sure that a new fourth party was 'strangled at birth'.

There was no doubt, however, about the public's support for a new breakaway social democrat party. Owen alone received over 3000 letters in the week after the launching of the Council for Social Democracy, the vast majority urging him to set up a new party as soon as possible. An opinion poll published in the *Sun* on 28 January suggested that a combined Liberal–social democratic party led by David Steel, Roy

TABLE 1: POLLS MEASURING PERCENTAGE SUPPORT FOR SOCIAL DEMOCRAT–LIBERAL ALLIANCE, MID–JANUARY TO END MARCH 1981

Published	18 Jan.[1]	28 Jan.[2]	1 Feb.[3]	9 Feb.[4]	–[5]	–[6]	–[7]	19 Mar.[8]	–[9]	–[10]
Conservative	29	26	25	24	29	28	28	25	23	21
Labour	33	22	32	30	29	32	29	27	29	30
Soc. dem.–Liberal	37	51	41	44	40	38	41	46	46	48

[1]ORC for Weekend World (fieldwork 12–14 Jan.)
[2]ASL for Sun (fieldwork 26 Jan.)
[3]NOP for Observer (fieldwork 18–29 Jan.)
[4]ORAC for The Times (fieldwork 31 Jan.–2 Feb.)
[5]NOP, unpublished (fieldwork 19–24 Feb.)
[6]NOP, unpublished (fieldwork 26 Feb.–3 March)
[7]NOP, unpublished (fieldwork 5–10 march)
[8]Gallup for Daily Telegraph (fieldwork 12–17 March)
[9]NOP, unpublished (fieldwork 12–17 March)
[10]NOP, unpublished (fieldwork 19–25 March)

Note: The answers are those given to a prompted question mentioning the possibility of a social democrat–Liberal alliance. In order to produce a fair comparison, the 'don't know' responses have been distributed proportionately among the parties.

Jenkins and Shirley Williams would win the support of over 50 per cent of the electorate. Admittedly the fact that the poll was conducted by telephone interviews almost certainly led to some distortion, but other polls conducted at about the same time were also giving a Liberal–social democratic party alliance a strong lead over both Labour and the Conservatives (see table 1).

The general atmosphere of excitement and near euphoria surrounding the launching of the Council for Social Democracy also spread to the SDA and the Association of Democratic Groups. On 31 January the two bodies held a joint rally, presided over by Lord George-Brown, the former Labour Foreign Secretary, who had a few days earlier become president of the SDA. They agreed to work together to build up grass-roots support for the new party which they saw as being not far off.

Among local councillors there had been a number of important defections from Labour both before and after the Wembley special conference. In Shrewsbury, John Wall, a Labour councillor for six years and a party member for thirty-three years, had resigned to set up a social democratic group on the council on 7 January. In Gloucester Michael Golder, a former Labour Parliamentary candidate for the city, and two Labour councillors had set up a social democratic group. In Bristol Roy Morris, deputy leader of the Labour group on the city council, resigned the party whip to sit as a social democrat. Several people in various parts of the country had already made it clear that they would be standing as social democrats in the county council elections in May.

The MPs associated with the Council for Social Democracy lost no time in consulting their constituency parties and letting them know their intentions. Owen led the way on 30 January, when he told his Plymouth, Devonport, party that he would not be seeking re-election as a Labour candidate at the next election. Others made similar statements to their local supporters. Mike Thomas even went to the length of sending postcards to all his constituents in Newcastle East to solicit their views about his action in joining the Council for Social Democracy. Of the first batch of replies he received, 75 per cent supported him, 9 per cent said that he should stay in the Labour Party and fight, 5 per cent said that he should stay if he could but go if he felt he must, and only 4 per cent expressed outright opposition.

Meanwhile, the 'Gang of Four' and their advisers were concentrating on building up support and a rudimentary organisational structure for the Council. Early in January Alec McGivan and Roger Liddle were given the task of arranging to place a half-page recruiting advertisement in the *Guardian* which would carry the names of a hundred leading supporters of the Council, to be chosen from the 8000 letters of support which had already been received following the Limehouse Declaration. The 'Declaration of a Hundred', as it came to be called, appeared on 5 February and included such well-known names as Steve Race, the musician and broadcaster, Janet Suzman, the actress, Lord Sainsbury, the head of the grocery chain, and Frank Chapple, General Secretary of the electricians' and plumbers' trade union. For a brief period the union's offices, which were located off Highbury fields in north London and were used by the Campaign for Labour Victory, were effectively the Council's headquarters. Alec McGivan, the CLV's secretary, acted as unofficial organiser of the new social democratic grouping.

On the evening before the *Guardian* advertisement appeared, an important meeting took place at Highbury of the steering committee of the CLV, the body which, more than any other, had urged social democrats to fight on within the Labour Party. Members of the group were evenly divided about whether the CLV should remain as it was or throw its weight behind the new breakaway movement, and a decision was taken to ballot the CLV's 5000 supporters in the country to see which option they preferred. That decision effectively marked the end of the CLV. The majority of those who had already written in to give their views had backed the idea of a breakaway. Alec McGivan resigned as secretary to devote himself full-time to organising the Council for Social Democracy.

On 5 February the Council set up a steering committee to direct its affairs. Together with the 'Gang of Four', McGivan and six MPs, it included David Marquand, Jim Daly and Dick Taverne. Other committees were later set up to oversee finance (Clive Lindley and David Sainsbury, another member of the grocery family, played leading roles in this), organisation, policy and communications. Two trustees were also appointed – Sir Leslie Murphy, a former chairman of the National Enterprise Board, and Lord Diamond, chairman of the Royal Commission on the Distribution of Income and Wealth and one of the founders of the Labour Committee for Europe.

Special care was taken to involve in the affairs of the Council leading figures in both the SDA and the Association of Democratic Groups. Douglas Eden, the secretary of the SDA, and Michael Barnes, founder of the west London democratic group, were appointed to the organisation committee. The degree to which these existing bodies became integrated with the new Council varied. The local democratic groups were on the whole happy to lose their individual identity and to become branches of the Social Democratic party when it was formed. Colin Phipps's group, for example, was reconstituted after 26 March as the West Midlands provisional area branch of the SDP. Michael Barnes joined the steering committee of the Kensington and Chelsea branch. The SDA, however, continued to maintain its separate identity, although all its members joined the Council and, later, the SDP.

The Social Democrats lost no time in finding an office close to the Houses of Parliament. Ian Wrigglesworth and Alec McGivan, who were charged with this task, had nearly taken a three-room suite in Strutton Ground, off Victoria Street. However, they found better premises on the second floor of a building in Queen Anne's Gate, opposite the back entrance to the Home Office. Its main attraction was that it offered room to expand. On 9 February Alec McGivan arrived with a broom to sweep out the three rooms there that the Council had taken initially and found 5000 replies from the *Guardian* advertisement piled up in sacks against the walls. Office tables and chairs were quickly and cheaply secured from a company that had gone bankrupt because of the recession – 'Mrs Thatcher's contribution to the party', as one social democrat put it – and within three weeks sixteen rooms were in use.

Initially, McGivan and his former assistant at the CLV, Sally Malnick, were the only full-time, paid staff of the Council. They were soon joined by John Lyttle, who was appointed press officer. Apart from them and a handful of agency secretaries, the offices were staffed entirely by volunteers, who had offered their services either directly to one of the 'Gang of Four' or in reply to the *Guardian* advertisment.

During the first couple of weeks of the Council's existence there continued to be some disagreement over how fast the Social Democrats should move. There was a general feeling that the final breakaway from Labour and the launch of the new party should take place at the end of May, although some influential voices urged that these events should not happen until after the Labour Party Conference in October. It was not long, however, before it became clear that the breakaway now had a momentum of its own and could not be delayed beyond the end of March.

TABLE 2   POLLS MEASURING PERCENTAGE SUPPORT FOR A SOCIAL DEMOCRATIC PARTY, 26 JANUARY TO MID–MARCH 1981

Published	29 Jan.[1]	9 Feb.[2]	7 Mar.[3]	19 Mar.[4]
Conservative	31	20	27	25.5
Labour	29	27	35	28
Liberal	11	16	13	13.5
Social democrat	27	25	23	31

[1]Marplan for *Guardian* (fieldwork 26 Jan.)
[2]ORAC for *The Times* (fieldwork 31 Jan.–2 Feb.)
[3]MORI for *Sunday Times* (fieldwork 19–23 Feb.)
[4]Gallup for *Daily Telegraph* (fieldwork 12–17 March)

Two factors hastened the formation of the new party. The first was the enormous interest shown in it by both the press and public, far more than any of the 'Gang' had ever antici-pated in their wildest dreams. Within five weeks of the Lime-house Declaration more than 25,000 letters urging a breakaway were received. Opinion polls carried out between the end of January and the end of March showed support running at between 23 and 31 per cent for a new social democratic party on its own, and at between 38 and 48 per cent for a Liberal–social democratic alliance (see tables 1 and 2). At the same time, pressure for a final break with the Labour Party was also coming from the MPs, who were finding their half-way position as members both of the party and of the Council increasingly uncomfortable and difficult to justify to their constituents.

What do you mean, can't we slow down a bit? We haven't even started the motor yet!

(Guardian, 2 February 1981)

The move towards a final breakaway began on 10 February with the resignation of Shirley Williams from Labour's NEC after ten consecutive years' membership. In an emotional letter to Ron Hayward, the party's General Secretary, she wrote, 'The party I loved and worked for over so many years no longer exists. . . . it is not the democratic socialist party that I joined.' The following day Mrs Williams confirmed that she would be leaving the Labour Party 'very soon'. Tom Bradley also resigned from the NEC a few days later. Bill Rodgers had already resigned from the Shadow Cabinet.

On 20 February Tom Ellis and Richard Crawshaw announced that they were resigning the Labour whip and would sit in the House of Commons as social democrats. The other ten MPs associated with the Council, who now also included John Cartwright, followed suit on 2 March. They took up their position on the Opposition front bench below the gangway, just in front of the Liberals and in the traditional haunt of left-wingers like Denis Skinner and Robert Cryer. Nine Labour peers also announced their defection to the social democrats on the same day. They were Lord Aylestone, Commonwealth Secretary between 1966 and 1967; Lady Burton of Coventry, a former Labour MP; Lord Diamond; Lord Donaldson of Kingsbridge, Minister for the Arts from 1976 to 1979; Lord Harris of Greenwich; Lord Kennet and Lord Walston, two former junior ministers and members of the European Parliament; Lord Winterbottom, a Government Whip from 1974 to 1978; and Lord Young of Dartington, President of the Consumers' Association.

On 16 March the still embryonic Social Democratic Party received a major boost when Christopher Brocklebank-Fowler, Conservative MP for Norfolk North-West, who had long been unhappy with Thatcherite policies, crossed the floor of the House of Commons to join it. Three days later Edward Lyons defected from the Labour benches, bringing the Social Democrats' strength in the commons to fourteen. During the next few days another nine peers announced they were joining the Social Democrats. They were Lord Sainsbury; Lord Bullock, the historian and former Vice-Chancellor of Oxford University; Lord Perry of Walton, the first Vice-chancellor of the Open University; Lord Ashby, Chancellor of Queen's University, Belfast; Lord Flowers, Rector of the Imperial College of Science and Technology; Lord Hunt, leader of the British expedition to Mount Everest in 1952; and three Scottish peers – Lord Kilmarnock, chief of the Clan Boyd in Scotland, Lord Taylor of Gryfe and Lord Wilson of Langside.

Meanwhile, it had been announced that the new party would be launched formally on 26 March, exactly two calendar months after the Limehouse Declaration. There was already £80,000 in the bank, most of it received in response to the *Guardian* advertisement; the polls were continuing to show enormous support for a Liberal–Social Democrat alliance, and every day brought a flood of letters of support and news of new defectors from the Labour Party. To the Liberals, the media and others who for months had been urging the social democrats to have the courage of their convictions and set up a new party, it had been an unconscionsable time coming. For those directly involved, however, it had all happened with breathtaking speed.

CHAPTER 6

What Sort of Party is the SDP?

The personalities, style and organisation of the party

In Britain all political parties of any significance are coalitions of widely different personalities and political styles. For all its youth, the SDP has already shown itself to be no exception to this rule. The dominant ethos of the new party is the progressive, concerned, metropolitan, middle-class liberalism represented by the Jenkinsites and the 'Gang of Four'. But there is also a strong undercurrent of conservative, almost reactionary, traditional, working-class labourism and antipathy towards the middle-class progressive left which reflects the attitudes of many of the party's grass-roots supporters and of those involved in the SDA. The contradictions and tensions between these two fundamentally different views of what the new party should be – a wholly new force of the 'radical centre', involving people previously committed to one of the existing parties or to none, or a Mark II Labour Party, appealing primarily to the traditional Labour vote and seeking to return to the golden days of Gaitskell and George Brown – have yet to be resolved. Already, however, it is possible to give at least a preliminary sketch of the style and composition of the party as it completes its first six months of existence.

Perhaps its most immediately striking feature is its lack of a single leader. At a time when British politics is becoming more and more American in style, as Prime Ministers become almost presidential in their roles and status and as elections are won and lost increasingly on the personalities of the leading figures involved, the new party has chosen, at least initially, to have a collective leadership. Strong hints have even been dropped that the principle of collective leadership may become permanent. Shirley Williams told a press conference in April that she thought the idea of a single leader might be dying, partly because of the danger of assassination attempts if too much power is concentrated in a single figure. David Owen even suggested, on the day after the launch of the SDP, that a single Prime Minister would not be essential to the running of a Social Democratic Government. It could equally well be led by a group of Ministers, who took it in turn to chair Cabinet meetings, just as the 'Gang of Four' take it in turn to chair the meetings of the SDP's steering committee which follow their own private lunch together every Monday afternoon.

It is quite conceivable that the collective leadership will be retained for some time, but it seems unlikely that it will be permanent. The whole matter will be put to the party membership to decide. One likely outcome is that the SDP will follow the example of several Continental parties and have one leader in Parliament and another in the country. The issue is a difficult one to resolve because of the role played by the 'Gang of Four'. They dominate the party in a way which is quite unique in British politics. For many people, both inside and outside the SDP, their personal dominance is altogether too pronounced – Sir Harold Wilson has called them 'a rather self-important group'. It is their faces which adorn the party's main recruiting leaflet and which look down benignly from the walls of the offices in Queen Anne's Gate, like icons in an Orthodox church. Yet there is no denying that the SDP is in many ways their creation. Certainly, their own personalities have played an important part in giving the party its distinctive style – or, rather, its various styles, since they do not themselves fit easily into a single mould.

Of the four, Roy Jenkins, as the ex-holder of two of the highest offices of state and a former President of the EEC, has the most *gravitas* and experience. At 60, he is also the oldest by nearly ten years, a fact which is reflected in the thoughtful and mellow quality of his speeches. He is also the most enthusiastic about the SDP's becoming a party of what he calls the 'radical centre' and the least happy about its becoming a revamped Labour Party. Appropriately for the biographer of Asquith and Sir Charles Dilke, he is at heart a radical Liberal who stresses constitutional and social reform and is distinctly hostile to the concept of socialism.

To judge from his manner, Jenkins might seem ideally cast to become the elder statesman of the SDP, content to take a backroom role and to let a younger person become leader. But he is not old in political terms, and his friends say that he would love to be the first British Social Democratic Prime Minister. His assets are his experience and his intelligence and the fact that throughout the late 1960s and early 1970s he was re- garded as leader by most of the social democrat Labour MPs who are now in the SDP. However, he is also saddled with a reputation for laziness and for a taste for good living. In the early days of the new party it was not an image that he did much to dispel. There was a well publicised incident on his train journey to launch the SDP in Wales when he was dis- turbed to find that he could not have a bottle of red wine with his breakfast. Given that it was 12.15 p.m. and the breakfast was having to stand in for the lunch that British Rail were unable to provide, it does not seem a wholly excessive or unreasonable request.[1] But his acceptance of the candidacy in the Warrington by-election, an act of some courage which won him much respect, suggested that he was making a conscious effort to shed his claret-drinking image and to prove himself if not quite one of the lads, then at least a serious politician who was not afraid of the rough and tumble of the market place.

Jenkins also has some claim to being regarded as the founder of the SDP. It started as a gleam in his eye as he sat in Brussels, reflecting on the political scene back home. His Dimbleby Lecture had first put the idea of a new party firmly before the public. Above all, perhaps, personal loyalty to him had played a major part in leading many social democrats to take the risky road out of the Labour Party. A significant proportion of those involved in creating the SDP were first and foremost Jenkins men. They included not just close friends and supporters out- side the House of Commons, like David Marquand, Dick Taverne, Lord Harris and Matthew Oakeshott, who had less to lose by joining the new venture, but also several of the sitting Labour MPs who defected to the Social Democrats. Bill Rod- gers had been Jenkins's Minister of State at the Treasury and Tom Bradley his Parliamentary Private Secretary (PPS). Ian Wrigglesworth had been his PPS at the Home Office, and Edward Lyons had been PPS to Rodgers and Taverne when they were his junior ministers. They all came over to the new party at least partly out of loyalty to their old leader.

Shirley Williams is the SDP's greatest electoral asset. She was the member of the 'Gang of Four' whom Michael Foot tried hardest to keep in the Labour fold and the one whom Labour MPs are most sorry to have lost. The loss is felt in both personal and political terms. Mrs Williams is by general consent the 'nicest' of the Gang – indeed, opinion polls show her consistently vying with David Steel as the most popular leading politician in the country.

Yet she is also in many ways the least suitable of the four to lead the SDP. She is inclined to be disorganised, muddled and chronically indecisive. Her reluctance to fight Warrington lost her considerable kudos within the party. She is also the most conservative in her thinking and the most rooted in traditional Labour philosophy. She remains firmly committed to the basic ideas of Beveridge and Keynes and is sceptical about proportional representation and decentralisation. Although issues, particularly Europe, played a part in detaching her from the Labour Party, the most important factor was what she saw as the destruction of the old values of fraternity by what she has called the 'fascists of the left'. As leader, she would be the most likely to make the SDP into a new-look Labour Party committed above all to the socialist goal of greater equality.

William Rodgers shares Shirley Williams's deep emotional attachment to the Labour Party and to its traditional working-class supporters. Like her, he found it painful to leave a movement in which he had been brought up and which he had served for so long. In many ways, his reasons for forming the new party are the most clear-cut. Since his early days as organiser of the Campaign for Democratic Socialism he had fought for the cause of social democracy in the Labour Party, and when the party finally turned its back on that cause, as he saw it, he left.

With only limited ministerial experience, he does not seem an obvious candidate for the leadership of the SDP. He is generally seen, rather, as a natural first lieutenant, loyal, competent and with considerable organisational abilities. However, that may be to underestimate his potential as a leader. He is more flexible than Shirley Williams and is anxious that the SDP should not become a Mark II Labour Party.

David Owen is the most intriguing and, on the face of it, the most surprising person to find among the leaders of the SDP. At 43 he is the youngest by some years. He is also the most ambitious. He enjoyed a meteoric rise to power in Callaghan's Government, becoming the youngest Foreign Secretary this century. In many ways he is more like an American than a British politician. Indeed, his American wife Debbie is said to see him as a Kennedy-style figure. Of the 'Gang of Three', he was the last to think about leaving the Labour Party but the most determined to go once he had considered the move.

Owen already effectively leads the party in Parliament, chairing the weekly meetings of Social Democrat MPs which decide what line should be taken in debates. He also did more than anyone else to bring most of those MPs into the party, having carefully courted them in meetings in his room throughout December and January. He certainly has the force-fulness to lead the Social Democrats, and his book *Face the Future*[2] gives him some claim to be regarded as a political thinker. As leader, he would almost certainly try to mould the SDP into a Continental-style party and would stress its youth and radicalism. In a characteristic note in his December strategy memorandum, he wrote, 'The whole key to success for any initiative is that it is new, different, young and fresh-looking. For every 60-year-old establishment figure, there must be a late thirties/early forties radical thinker and far more than just a token woman.'

Owen is almost obsessive about the principle of one man, one vote, which was his sticking-point as regards staying in the Labour Party. He enjoys the new possibilities which tech-nology offers to the practice of politics in the 1980s and predicts that the SDP will use sophisticated computer question-naires to sound out the opinions of its members. His speeches are full of praise for the achievements of the Scandinavian countries and the successes of European social democracy. He insists that the SDP must be clearly to the left of centre, and of all the 'Gang' he has the least time for the Liberals. His liabilities in the leadership stakes are his impatience, his rather cold manner and his reputation for being rather ruthless and arrogant.

If there are differences in style and emphasis between these four leaders, they also have much in common. They are all

Oxbridge graduates (Owen again being the odd man out, with a Cambridge education) and share a broadly progressive, intellectual, middle-class view of life. Jenkins and Rodgers are grammar-school boys, the sons of a Welsh miners' MP and a Liverpool Corporation clerk respectively. David Owen, the son of a well-to-do general practitioner, has a solidly professional and public-school background, while Shirley Williams enjoyed an essentially upper-middle-class, if unconventional, upbringing as the daughter of the writer Vera Brittain and her husband Sir George Catlin.

All four practise a rather low-key, almost passionless, style of politics, which puts more stress on quiet, rational persuasion than on oratorical fervour. They are inclined to treat their speeches slightly like papers to university seminar groups and favour tightly argued academic disquisitions of a slightly dry nature on such subjects as the Brandt Report, European social democracy and decentralisation. None speaks as though he had fire in his belly. For all the enthusiasm that the launch has engendered, SDP meetings do not have the revivalist, almost inspirational quality of Labour and Liberal rallies or even some Conservative gatherings. There are no great oratorical fireworks in the manner of Michael Foot or Margaret Thatcher, Tony Benn or Michael Heseltine. Instead the mood is cooler and more detached, rather as one imagines it is at gatherings of the European social democratic parties.

This quality of calm reasonableness extends to many of the SDP's leading activists and to most of its fourteen original MPs. So, incidentally, does a middle-class, Oxbridge background. Dick Taverne, David Marquand and Michael Barnes were at Oxford in the early 1950s. Roger Liddle and Matthew Oakeshott were contemporaries there as undergraduates in the mid-1960s and were respectively secretary and chairman of the University Labour Club (coincidentally, the very offices held by Bill Rodgers and Shirley Williams when they were at Oxford together in the early 1950s). Both stayed on in Oxford as city councillors in the early 1970s, when they met and worked with two undergraduates, Alec McGivan and Richard Newby, the latter of whom gave up a promising career in the Civil Service to become secretary and researcher to the Social Democrat MPs.

Among the original MPs there are two fairly distinct groups. One, which is composed of those with predominantly working-class, non-Oxbridge backgrounds, will be considered later in this chapter. The other group, which is made up of John Horam, John Roper, Robert Maclennan, Richard Crawshaw, Neville Sandelson and Christopher Brocklebank-Fowler,

'There's nothing in the phone book under Social Democrats – perhaps if you want to join them you have to be an MP first.'
(*Guardian, 17 March 1981*)

shares the broadly middle-class outlook and experience of the 'Gang of Four'. Of those six MPs, five are Oxbridge graduates, four were at public schools and three are barristers. The only one with a working-class background is John Horam, whose father was a fitter and whose mother was a newsagent. The five who came over from Labour share a quiet, almost diffident intellectual manner, which always separated them from many of their blunter and more rumbustious colleagues on the Labour benches.

Many of the earliest recruits to the party had the same characteristics. It was significant that there was more than a fair share of academics among the SDP's first list of distinguished supporters. The 'Declaration of a Hundred' in the *Guardian* was signed by three former university vicechancellors, Lord Bullock of Oxford, Lord Perry of the Open University, and Sir Charles Carter of Lancaster; by three leading academic economists, Sir Alec Cairncross, Professor James Meade and Professor Frank Hahn; by Lord Flowers, the Rector of Imperial College, London; and by sixteen university teachers. Numerous other academics joined the party in its early weeks, and it was no coincidence that Oxford and Cambridge provided two of the earliest and most flourishing provisional branches.

Students also flocked to the SDP in considerable numbers. At the beginning of March Social Democrat candidates swept the board in student union elections at the traditionally left-wingdominated London School of Economics. Similar results followed at other universities, and a Student Campaign for Realignment was set up to rally support for a Liberal–Social Democrat alliance. By the middle of June the Campaign already had more than 1000 members in over forty institutions of higher education.

The new party also gained a significant number of recruits from the quasi-academic world of research institutes. Indeed, the largest of these, the Policy Studies Institute, Britain's nearest equivalent to the American Brookings Institute, almost seemed to qualify for designation as the Social Democratic think-tank, so enthusiastic was the involvement of several of its leading members in the SDP. Both the chairman of its research and management committee, Sir Charles Carter, and its Director of Administration, Richard Davies, were among the signatories to the 'Declaration of a Hundred', as was a leading member of its council, Jean Floud. Dr Roger Morgan, one of its senior members of staff and a leading authority on European social democracy, was an early recruit. Significantly, perhaps, Shirley Williams has been a part-time professorial fellow of the

Institute and has used its offices as a base since she lost her seat in the 1979 General Election.

Leading figures in other research institutes were also among the SDP's earliest and most enthusiastic supporters. Dick Taverne is Director of the Institute of Fiscal Studies, which occupies part of the ground floor of the Policy Studies Institute's building in Westminster. William Plowden, Director of the Royal Institute of Public Administration, was an early recruit, as was Keith Kyle of the Royal Institute of International Affairs at Chatham House. A slightly different kind of research body, the Consumers' Association, was represented by Lord Young, its President, and by Eirlys Roberts, the former editor of *Which?*, who were both among the signatories of the 'Declaration of a Hundred'.

Members of the professions and those involved in serious journalism and writing were also well to the fore among the first recruits. As was pointed out at the beginning of Chapter 3, the first specialist group set up by the new party was composed of solicitors and barristers. The moving spirit behind this group, which within a month had more than 200 members, was another Jenkinsite, Anthony Lester, who had served as special adviser to the Home Secretary from 1974 to 1976. Among the writers who signed the 'Declaration of a Hundred' were Anthony Sampson, author of *The Anatomy of Britain*, who subsequently outlined his views for his regular readers in the *New Statesman* in an article entitled 'Why I am a Social Democrat', and Polly Toynbee, the *Guardian* columnist, who succeeded in sparking off a lengthy correspondence in that paper about whether it was possible, as she claimed it was, to be a supporter both of the SDP and of unilateral nuclear disarmament.

Similarly middle-class, professional types predominated among volunteers who worked at the new party's headquarters during the months following the launch. The receptionist at Queen Anne's Gate, Michael Starkey, was a former private secretary in the Foreign Office and bursar of Harrow School, who had written to Shirley Williams offering his services to the Social Democrats in no matter how menial a capacity. The telephone was quite likely to be answered by Lady Thomson of Monifieth, wife of George (now Lord)

Thomson, the former EEC Commissioner. Morning coffee was often served by a former deputy speaker of the House of Commons, Richard Crawshaw, and messages were taken by the president of the Cambridge University Students Union, Ian Wright.

Celia Goodhart, a history teacher and wife of a leading QC, was in charge of sorting out offers of help, and Ruth Levy, a free-lance designer who had been converted to the idea of a new party by Jenkins's Dimbleby Lecture, was in charge of the volunteers. In the days leading up to the launch she had nearly thirty of them engaged in opening letters, counting cheques and packing up boxes of leaflets. The youngest helper was Dominic Lees, a 16-year-old pupil at Bedales School, who had become a Social Democrat after hearing a lecture by David Owen. The oldest, Arthur Pulham, a 71-year-old retired printer from the Stationery Office, had left the Labour Party after forty years chiefly because of 'the control that the party caucuses are now imposing on MPs'.[3]

The inaugural meetings of the first provisional SDP branches in London also had a distinctly middle-class atmosphere. It was significant that some of the first branches to be formed were in the fashionable areas of Kensington and Chelsea, where Michael Barnes and Norman Hart, the co-founder of the Labour Committee for Europe, were the moving spirits; Lambeth, where Roger Liddle took the leading role; and Camden, where a complex organisational structure was created, with Ben Stoneham, the former treasurer of the CLV, as overall convenor, Ernest Wistrich, director of the European Movement, in charge of publicity and Keith Kyle in charge of policy. Among the fund-raising activities suggested in the first newsletter of the Camden branch was a plate supper for members at the Reform Club.

It was hardly surprising that the SDP's critics chose to portray it as a party of trendy media folk and well-to-do élitists. Tony Benn saw its natural constituency as Fleet Street, Television Centre and the City. Roy Hattersley said that it stood for 'a set of middle-class platitudes, the need to build a Britain free for credit card holders'. Another Labour MP described its members to the *Guardian* journalist Simon Hoggart as 'London intellectuals surveying a declining Britain from the comfort of Holland Park'.[4]

There was more than a grain of truth in those jibes. The fact was that the SDP did have an enormous initial appeal for that new constituency which had grown up in the 1970s, the vaguely progressive, *Guardian*-reading middle class which worked in education, communications, technology and the so-called caring professions and was concerned about the

'We shouldn't have any more defectors to the Social Democrats – I've ordered everyone to hand in their Access and Barclaycards.'
(Guardian, *19 March 1981*)

Third World, the environment, the decentralisation of government and staying in Europe. As Bill Rodgers was fond of pointing out, the party had attracted 'the thinking public'. The SDP was well aware that its initial support was likely to come predominantly from this group. Why else would it have placed its first advertisement in their house journal, the *Guardian*?

For this new class the SDP represented something that no political party had ever given them before. It seemed to speak in their language and to echo their concerns in a way that previously only non-political institutions had done. Perhaps the organisations which had come closest to representing their views were, in fact, the Churches, through the liberal social gospel which they had preached during the 1960s and 1970s. As Clifford Longley, religious affairs correspondent of *The Times* put it, 'The political face of British Christianity has for at least half a generation been "social democratic" and is still tending that way.'[5] Part of the appeal of the SDP for the concerned and still nominally Christian middle classes was undoubtedly the fact that in its commitment to the Third World, human rights, multi-racial harmony and greater equality coupled with respect for individual liberty, it offered a secularised version of the doctrine being disseminated by the liberal Church establishment.

Politically, these new recruits came from a variety of backgrounds. Several were past members of the Conservative or Liberal parties, and a small but significant minority had been involved with the Ecology Party and other fringe groups. A much greater number came from what might be called the Fabian wing of the Labour party. Indeed, at one stage there was a feeling that the Fabian Society might be captured as a think-tank for the Social Democrats, since so many of its members had defected to the new party. However, a ballot of the whole membership of the Fabian Society decided that only those eligible to join the Labour Party could be full members of the Society, and those who had joined the SDP were forced to leave. The only political group from which the new party did not appear to recruit in significant numbers was the far left, although there was one notable defector from the Communist Party in Sue Slipman, a former president of the National Union of Students.

Many — indeed, probably the majority — of the new recruits had never been members of any political party before. Typically, they had voted Liberal in 1974 but did not feel any close identification with any of the old parties. A prominent member of this group was Bernard Doyle, a 40-year-old civil engineer and director of Booker McConnell, the large engineering and

trading company, who was chosen from more than 320 appli-
cants to be the SDP's first chief executive. His sympathies had
been with the Liberals, although he had never felt that they
were getting anywhere. He applied for the job, he said, because
he felt the new party offered the chance of busting the political
system, 'and that is the sort of chance that only comes every
fifty years or so.'[6]

The reasons which people gave for joining varied according
to their own political backgrounds. Former Conservatives
tended to stress their antipathy for Margaret Thatcher's harsh
economic policies, and particularly for the March budget.
Suzanne Jones, the mayor of Bridgend, in South Wales, and
one of the first Tory councillors to defect to the SDP, summed
up a common feeling about the new party when she said,
'There is not so much bureaucracy with them as with the other
parties. They are not going to let the unions run the country.
They are more in line with middle-of-the-road people.'[7]

Those coming from the Liberals and the smaller parties were
particularly attracted to the SDP's commitment to decentralisation. That was the major factor in the conversion of two of the
leading figures in the Cornish branch of the new party, Jenni
Thomson, a former Ecology Party member, and Len Trunan, a
former Parliamentary candidate and secretary of the Cornish
nationalist party, Mebyon Keinow.

Among the middle-class Labour defectors the reasons most
often cited for joining the SDP were the gradual drift to the left
and the constitutional decisions taken at Blackpool and
Wembley. Christopher Cousins, a solicitor in Weymouth,
Dorset, and a Labour Party member since the age of 16, had
been 'rudely awakened to the power that existed in the hands
of a few trade union leaders' when he went to the 1979 Labour
Party Conference. Wembley had been the breaking-point for
him, 'since I tend to the view that parties should be run by their
members'. For David Mason, a Methodist minister and community worker in Lewisham and a former Labour Parliamentary candidate,

discontent with the party had been rumbling away for two or three
years. I felt we could put our own house in order but the Wembley
Conference was the last straw. What really pushed me out is the
whole shift away from representative democracy and the attempt to
mandate elected representatives by party caucuses.[8]

Among those who had joined the SDP with no previous political affiliations, the most frequently cited reasons in the letters which often accompanied their membership applications were the desire to see the end of polarised and adversarial politics and hope for the establishment of a truly classless party in Britain. For all of these middle-class recruits the SDP represented a break with old-style party politics. They envisaged it as a grouping of the 'radical centre' and not in any sense as a Mark II Labour Party.

The evidence of opinion polls tends to confirm a middle-class bias in the early support for the SDP. A MORI poll at the end of April found, in answer to the standard unprompted question about how respondents would vote in a General Election, that 19 per cent of those in social class AB (managerial and professional) supported the Social Democrats, compared with 15 per cent of C1s (white-collar workers), 10 per cent of C2s (skilled manual workers) and only 7 per cent of DEs (semi-skilled and unskilled workers). A prompted question reminding respondents of the existence of the Social Democratic Party produced the following anwers in terms of percentage support for the main parties from each social class:

	ABs	C1s	C2s	DEs
Social Democrat	30	24	23	18
Conservative	44	38	20	18
Labour	13	21	39	48
Liberal	13	14	14	13

The same poll also found that, contrary to what many people thought, the highest concentration of support for the SDP was not among the young but among the 35 to 44 age group. That finding tends to confirm the thesis of one former Labour activist in Plymouth, who told me that she thought the SDP was capturing the support of what for Labour was a lost generation, those born between 1935 and 1945, who were too young to have experienced the Depression and too old to have been radicalised in the late 1950s and early 1970s.

Though there is a distinct middle-class bias in the initial members and supporters of the SDP, it is not as pronounced as some have made out, and it is likely to become less marked as the party becomes more established. Those who joined in the early days needed to have cheque books, if not the much publicised credit cards, and the motivation and confidence either to telephone or to write to party headquarters. As branches are formed and house-to-house canvassing takes place, more working-class are likely to join.

There is already an important element in the new party which is very different in background and outlook from the professional *Guardian* readers who packed the inaugural meetings of the Camden and Lambeth branches. In the Midlands and the North the SDP has attracted many supporters who are solidly working-class and have little time for the progressive liberalism of Hampstead and Kennington or for the pro-Europeanism of the 'Gang of Four'. They have joined the new party not out of any great ideological commitment to its policies but because of their personal experience of the take-over of the Labour Party by young middle-class left-wingers. They are more inclined to see the SDP as a Mark II Labour Party.

To a certain extent, this group is represented in Parliament by Tom Bradley, John Cartwright, Tom Ellis, Edward Lyons, Mike Thomas and Ian Wrigglesworth. In their background these MPs are very different from the other six Social Democrats mentioned above. None of them went to public school or Oxbridge, and only three are university graduates. Cartwright comes from a lower-middle-class family in Surrey. The others were all brought up in working-class homes in the industrial areas of Britain. Ellis and Bradley were both miners, Lyons the son of a Jewish tailor in Leeds, Wrigglesworth the son of a Tyneside fitter and Thomas the son of a heating engineer from the same area. They were all much more in the mainstream of the Labour movement than the other group of Social Democrat MPs, four of them having either trade union or Co-Operative Party sponsorship. Although they are strongly pro-European, they tend to be less enamoured of the centre party idea and more hostile towards the Liberals.

Typical of this group is David Elford, who joined the new party at the end of March, after fifteen years as chairman or vice-chairman of the Falmouth and Cambourne Constituency Labour Party. While others on the Cornwall steering committee of the SDP joined because of their ecological and decentralist views, he had much more down-to-earth reasons: 'The Militant Tendency are very strong down here. They are dedicated Marxists and they just made things intolerable in the Labour Party. I think the Social Democrats have got more common sense. They will tread more quietly.'[9]

Six Labour councillors in the London borough of Islington, who resigned the party whip in March to form themselves into the largest Social Democratic group on any local authority, moved over for much the same reasons. The immediate cause of their defection was the selection of a left-winger as candidate for Islington North in the Greater London Council elections and the take-over by the left of the executive of the local Labour Party. But there were also more deep-seated reasons, which are worth examining as they were to be found in many other traditional Labour strongholds.

Islington displays in particularly striking form the conflicts which have built up over the last twenty years in many local Labour parties. The fifty-strong Labour group on the council is divided into two clear factions. The larger one, from which the six Social Democrat defectors came, is made up predominantly of working-class, middle-aged men, locally born and bred, who are conservative in their outlook and policies. Their main opposition (there are only two Tories on the Council) comes from a group of younger, middle-class men and women who moved into Islington with the 'gentrification' of the borough in the 1960s and 1970s and who are of a more left-wing persuasion.

Gradually, the second group, which is appalled by what it regards as the first's lack of progressive policies and lack of concern for the under-privileged, has won more and more influence in the local Labour party. It now looks as though many of the older working-class councillors may not secure nomination as candidates in the 1982 local elections. Seen from one perspective, those of them who defected to the SDP were simply fleeing in the face of defeat. Their day was over, and they should have bowed out gracefully. However, they see themselves as victims of a deliberately orchestrated campaign by the left, which has involved packing meetings and other manipulations of the party constitution.

At the root of their defection is their feeling that the Labour Party is no longer their party. As Jim Evans, their leader, put it:

We used to have a lot of old people come to meetings. They had come for years although they didn't always have the education to put over their views. The middle-class student types just laughed at them and mocked them, and so they stopped coming. In the old days we had meetings and then went off to the pub afterwards. These new people started coming in with sandwiches and flasks and the meetings went on until two or three in the morning.[10]

If Roy Jenkins is the hero of the middle-class intellectuals who see the SDP as a new party of the 'radical centre', then Lord George-Brown is perhaps the patron saint of the working-class traditionalists who see it more as a resurrection of the old-style Labour Party, purged of its recent contamination by the left. It is no coincidence that he should be president of the SDA, the body which comes nearest to representing this second brand of social democracy. It was also significant that although all the members of the SDA joined the SDP when it was formed, they maintained their separate identity; the SDA was kept on as a grouping to fight the county council elections in May. Its leaders stress their working-class roots and are noticeably hostile towards middle-class intellectuals. Douglas Eden, for example, sees the left as

a middle-class self-appointed vanguard of the working class telling people what's good for them. . . . The traditional Labour Party we supported was one where working class people could get to the top of it; now it is just a vehicle for ideology.[11]

Significantly, when Eden stood as a Social Democrat candidate in Islington in the Greater London Council elections in May, he was strongly supported by Lord George-Brown. His appeal was based on a return to old-style Labour values rather than the creation of a new, radical, fresh centre party. 'The official Labour Party is the party of Arthur Scargill and Wedgwood Benn,' his election address ran. 'It is not the Labour Party you may have voted for in the past. A vote for Eden is a vote for the traditional values of trusted Labour leaders like Clem Attlee, Hugh Gaitskell and George Brown.'

There are obvious tensions between these two different groups in the SDP. They surfaced even before the party was born in the division of opinion that we noted in chapter 5 between those who wanted an early launch based on the development of grass-roots groups in the country and those who wanted to wait until there was a significant breakaway at Westminster. To a certain extent, that division has continued ever since, with those on what might be called the SDA, working-class, provincial wing of the party feeling that the 'Gang of Four' and their supporters are too London-orientated and concentrate too much on Parliament and not enough on the country as a whole.

The different attitudes taken to the May county council elections by the SDA and the SDP steering committee revealed a similar division of opinion between the two main elements in the party. The SDA, together with other democratic Labour groups which had been active for some time, were keen to field Social Democratic candidates in the election. The 'Gang of Four', however, regarded it as too soon after the launch of the new party to mount a nationwide campaign and considered the risks of a poor result to be too high to justify putting up candidates. In the event, about a hundred Social Democrat candidates stood in the elections, including eight put up specifically by the SDA in London, but not one of them was endorsed by, or received any help from, the SDP.

The clash over the local elections put a severe strain on the already rather delicate relations between the SDA and the SDP. Douglas Eden was temporarily removed from the SDP's organisation committee while he was a candidate, and Jim Daly, who was to have been SDA candidate in Paddington, stepped down after pressure was put on him by his fellow members of the SDP steering committee. Privately, leading members of the SDA complained about the élitism of the 'Gang of Four' and about their public endorsement of Liberal candidates when they had gone out of their way to make it clear they were not endorsing those standing as Social Democrats. On the other side, there was a feeling in Queen Anne's Gate that the SDA were more of a hindrance than a help, and that some of the candidates who were putting up as Social Democrats would do the image of the party no good.

The organisation of the new party was another subject on which opinions differed. The 'Gang of Four' and their supporters deliberately decided to make the structure of the SDP different from that of existing political parties. First, there was the collective leadership. Then there was the appointment of a chief executive, a position unknown in the other parties, which smacked of the business world. A conscious effort was made to provide the finances for the party almost entirely from individual members' subscriptions and to avoid either trade union affiliation fees or donations from companies. In organising the party in the country, the traditional unit of the Parliamentary constituency was eschewed in favour of a larger area, the metropolitan or shire county, or the borough in the case of London. As we have already noted, the time-honoured practice of holding a week-long conference by the seaside was dropped in favour of a 'rolling' conference starting in Perth, continuing in Bradford and ending up in London. Even more radically, hints were dropped that party policy and elections would be decided by regular postal ballots of members, made possible by the computerised technology which had been such a feature of the SDP's launch.

All this may have seemed very exciting to the media folk of Camden, but to some of the SDP's other supporters it seemed too much of a trendy gimmick. They were worried that the party leadership was devoting too much time and attention to its image and not enough to building a solid grass-roots base. There was also a suspicion that the postal balloting might not be quite as democratic as it sounded. Did it not have many of the same drawbacks as government by referendum, to which the 'Gang of Four' had been so much opposed during the battle over the EEC in the mid-1970s? Lurking at the back of many people's minds was an even more serious worry about the position of the members of the 'Gang' themselves. Would they submit their own leadership to the party members? They talked an awful lot about 'one man, one vote' and democracy, but not one of them had been elected. None of them had been notable in the past for always following the wishes of rank-and-file members of their party. Indeed, they had left the Labour Party because they would not accept decisions democratically taken by its Conference. Was there any reason to think that they would change their spots now?

Relations with the Liberals, the biggest single political question the new party faced, also proved to be a divisive issue. Broadly, those whose links with the Labour Party had been weakest and who inclined most towards the centre party idea were strongly pro-Liberal and favoured as close an alliance as possible with the Liberal Party, while those who came from traditional Labour areas and backgrounds had less time for the Liberals and were considerably cooler about an alliance.

There were perceptible differences on the issue within the 'Gang of Four'. Roy Jenkins was by far the most pro-Liberal. He had a high personal regard for David Steel and, as we have seen, was himself in many ways a Liberal in all but name. His close friends and supporters, like David Marquand and Dick Taverne, were also strongly in favour of an early alliance and, if necessary, concessions to the Liberals to secure it. The other three were less enthusiastic about an alliance, although all saw the necessity for one. Shirley Williams had never had very much time for the Liberals; Bill Rodgers had been unimpressed by their performance in the Lib.–Lab. pact; and David Owen, while aware of their strength in his own West Country, was inclined to dismiss them and to forget to mention them in his speeches.

The Social Democrat MPs were also split. The more middle-class, intellectual group was strongly pro-Liberal, and those with more traditional Labour roots were much less enthusiastic about an alliance. Their attitudes depended partly on their experiences in their own constituencies. Both Richard Crawshaw, in the strongly Liberal area of Liverpool, and Bob Maclennan, who had won his seat from the Liberals, had considerable respect for them. On the other hand, Ian Wrigglesworth and Mike Thomas, representing solid Labour areas in the North-East, where the Liberals had made little impact, were inclined to be much more dismissive.

The argument between the two groups flared up at a meeting of the SDP's MPs and steering committee on 7 April. Shirley Williams reported on a conversation she had had with David Steel while they were climbing a mountain at Königswinter the week before. By the time they had finished the walk, they had agreed on the need for an early alliance and on how it could be achieved. When their plan was put to the meeting, several of the MPs expressed their fear that they were being bounced into an agreement with the Liberals and demanded that a higher price should be exacted from their prospective partners. Further discussion of the matter was postponed. Talks with the Liberals moved slowly thereafter, with the first formal meeting of representatives of the two parties taking place on 20 May and a joint statement of principles being issued on 16 June. Even after this differences of opinion persisted in the SDP about the desirability, the nature and the extent of further dealings with the Liberals over arrangements for fighting elections.

Behind all these conflicts lies a fundamental division between those who see the SDP essentially as an entirely new force in British politics and those who see it rather as a party which will rekindle the spirit of the old-style Gaitskellite Labour Party. The former is undoubtedly the dominant view at the moment. It is held by the 'Gang of Four', which, while it stresses that the SDP is a left-of-centre party which must cut deep into the traditional Labour vote, ardently hopes that the party will not recruit its members primarily from among old Labour Party Stalwarts who want to fight again what they see as the battles of the past.

There is, on the other hand, a substantial minority who feel that the party is in danger of going too much for a trendy, new, centre-party image, and that it would do better to model itself more on the traditional Labour Party. That view was cogently expressed in a letter to *The Times* on 5 June by Tom Ellis:

Nor does a determination to reject the practices of the Labour Party become anything other than silly if, in fact, it results in no more than administrative decisions about not having an annual conference because Labour has one, or not basing local parties on the constituencies because Labour does so, or disparaging local party members who were formerly active workers in the old parties.

It is too early to say how this conflict will resolve itself and what sort of party will eventually emerge. At this early stage the middle-class 'radical centrists' seem to have the upper hand, and those who want a Mark II Labour Party are in the minority. It may well be, however, that the SDP will end up as a coalition between these two groups and a compromise between the two kinds of party that they stand for. As Roy Jenkins wrote some years ago, 'A social democratic party without deep roots in the working-class movement would quickly fade into an unrepresentative intellectual sect.'[12]

CHAPTER 7

What Does the SDP Stand For?

The policies and philosophy of the Social Democrats

When a lady approached David Owen on the steps of Southampton Civic Hall on the day of the SDP's launch and asked him what was in the new party's manifesto, he replied, 'Look, love, if you want a manifesto, go and join one of the other parties.'[1] The 'Gang of Four' has so far deliberately avoided committing itself to detailed policies. It maintains that to do so before the party membership has been given a chance to discuss or vote on them would be élitist and undemocratic, and that anyway it wants to get away from what Roy Jenkins called at the launch 'the disease of manifestoitis'.

This approach has both its strengths and its weaknesses. It is certainly true that the major parties, not least the Liberals, tend to saddle themselves with far too much detailed policy and to cram their manifestos full of specific promises on all manner of subjects. There is a lot to be said for a party which reverts to the nineteenth-century tradition of having virtually no manifesto at all but stands on certain broad principles and on its ability and common sense. However, any political group needs some clear statement of philosophy and policy to give it an identity recognisable both by its supporters and by the electorate; otherwise there is a danger that no one will know what it stands for. There are already signs that this problem is affecting the SDP. A MORI poll at the end of April found, for example, that almost as many people thought it was the policy of the new party to take Britain out of the EEC as to keep Britain in.

The SDP issued brief statements of policy both at the time of the Limehouse Declaration and on the launch day of the party proper. Although they are often so vague that they border on the platitudinous, it is worth quoting them in full as a guide to the party's overall philosophy and policy. First, the statement of principles which originally formed part of the Limehouse Declaration and was later amended for inclusion in the interim rules of the SDP:

> The SOCIAL DEMOCRATIC PARTY exists to create an open, classless and more equal society which rejects prejudices based upon sex, race or religion.
> - The Party aims to strengthen Britain's economy and is committed to fostering a healthy public sector and a healthy private sector without frequent frontier changes.
> - It seeks to eliminate poverty and promote greater equality without stifling enterprise or imposing bureaucracy from the centre.
> - It recognises the need for the innovating strength of a competitive economy with a fair distribution of rewards.
> - It seeks to encourage competitive public enterprise, co-operative ventures and profit sharing.
> - It supports the greatest practicable degree of decentralisation of decision-making in industry and government, together with an effective and practical system of democracy at work.
> - It is committed to fairer systems of elections at every level and to strengthening parliamentary democracy.
> - It is concerned to improve public and community services and their responsiveness to people's needs.
> - It seeks to attain high employment and restrain inflation.
> - It intends that Britain will play a full and constructive role within the framework of the European community, NATO, the United Nations and the Commonwealth, in the belief that within such a multilateral framework lies the hope of negotiating international agreements covering arms control and disarmament and the prospect of grappling effectively with the poverty of the Third World.

Second, the slightly fuller statement entitled 'Twelve Tasks for Social Democrats', which was published on 26 March 1981 to coincide with the SDP's launch:

1 Breaking the mould
Britain needs a reformed and liberated political system without the pointless conflict, the dogma, the violent lurches of policy and the class antagonisms that the two old parties have fostered.

2 Fair elections
The present 'winner takes all' system of electing MPs is unfair to the voters and opens the door to extremism, whether of left or right. We

need a sensible system of proportional representation in which every vote really counts.

3 *A consistent economic strategy*

To secure Britain's livelihood in the nineties, we need a consistent economic strategy in the eighties, one that is not disrupted every few years by a political upheaval. The opportunity provided by our temporary oil wealth should not be frittered away, but should be used to invest in new industries and new jobs and to rehabilitate the regions. Such an investment programme in the vital areas of industry, communications, public transport and the environment must be backed up by an incomes policy flexible enough to last and which will reduce the conflict between higher employment and lower inflation.

4 *Employment policies*

We are determined to create new jobs and reduce unemployment, by introducing a training programme for school-leavers and a modern apprenticeship system, by encouraging small and medium-sized businesses which provide job opportunities, and by supporting schemes to conserve energy, raw materials and other scarce resources.

5 *A mixed economy*

There must be positive support for a mixed economy without constant Conservative sniping at the public sector or repeated Labour threats to private enterprise. Public and private firms should flourish side by side without frequent frontier changes. There should be democracy at work, with profit sharing, co-operatives and local enterprise. We need trade unions representative of their members as a whole, and a responsive management willing to inform and consult with its workforce. Both trade unions and management must be fully aware of their responsibilities to the whole community.

6 *A fair distribution of wealth*

We recognise the capacity of market forces to create new wealth, a capacity unmatched by any centrally controlled economy in the world. We must also recognise that market forces, left to themselves, distribute rewards extremely unfairly. So we must strike a balance between rewarding enterprise and effort and distributing its products fairly. The State should lean towards greater equality; but if it intervenes oppressively it will damage individual liberty and diminish the nation's wealth.

7 *Decentralisation*

Decisions should more often be made at local level, involving people affected by them. The 'men in Whitehall', whether Ministers or civil servants, do not always know best. Every citizen should be able to find out about, and challenge, executive decisions. Parliament must be free from the control of party machines, and should exercise more effective power over Government Departments. The Second Chamber needs to be reformed but not abolished. We wish to see a practical and acceptable devolution of power to the nations and regions of Britain.

8 Welfare and the community
We are pledged to improve the quality of our health services, our housing and the education of our children, and to make these and other community services more responsive to people's needs, not least in the inner cities. The welfare state should be less bureaucratic, concerned above all with the well-being of individuals.

9 A better environment
The environment of this densely populated country must be protected and cared for. If we are to ensure a decent environment for our children we must, in each generation, be prepared to pay some economic cost.

10 Equality for women
Despite recent changes, women are still not treated in our society as equal citizens. Women who work in the home have rights which should be respected and need good family support services. Those who work outside the home should have equal pay and equal opportunity. The spirit of existing laws should be implemented; positive further action is necessary.

11 A society for all
We live in a multi-racial society, but we have signally failed to offer equal opportunities to all its members. There should be no discrimination on grounds of race, colour or religion, or against any minority group. All our people should have equal rights, including the fundamental rights of citizensnhip.

12 International co-operation
Britain should co-operate in the world and not retreat into sour isolation. We need our friends in a dangerous world, which means playing our full part in the European Community and in NATO, vigorously pursuing multilateral but not unilateral disarmament. We will not insulate ourselves from the hunger and poverty of the Third World. Without imaginative generosity, which marches alongside far-sighted self-interest, we shall not only frustrate the hopes of the developing world, but undermine our own long-term prosperity.

The task for Social Democrats is to make Britain successful and tolerant at home, self-confident and far-sighted abroad.

It is rather difficult, and perhaps also a little unfair, to try to establish what the SDP stands for on the basis of those two rather thin statements. Fortunately for all concerned, they have been amplified by two more substantial treatises by two of the founding figures of the new party, David Owen's 550-page book *Face the Future*,[2] which was rushed out by its publisher to appear just four days after the Limehouse Declaration, and Shirley Williams's rather slimmer volume, *Politics is for People*,[3] which was published in April. Taking points from those two books, as well as from the two statements printed above, it is possible to form an impression of the party's philosophy and policies.

Perhaps the first aspect of both the books and the briefer statements to strike the reader is the excitement of their language and their stress on the new and radical. This comes over very clearly in Mrs Williams's book, where she says: 'Politicians, and in particular those like me who believe in social democracy, will have to make a quantum jump in their thinking, a leap to a new approach, if the West is to move forward from the achievements of the post-war years.'[4]

It comes, perhaps, as a slight disappointment, after this promise of something new and radical, to find that the clearest policy commitments of all are to those now rather old and distinctly unradical institutions, the EEC and NATO. The fact is, of course, that it was the support of the 'Gang of Four' for the Common Market and their opposition to unilateral disarmament and neutralism which had long set them and their supporters apart from much of the rest of the Labour Party and eventually led them to leave. So it is hardly surprising that they should take those two policies with them into their new party.

Of all the SDP's policies, commitment to Britain's continued membership of the EEC is the one most widely and strongly held by the leadership and activists. Unfortunately, as we shall discover in the next chapter, it is also the one for which there is least enthusiasm among their supporters. In the higher echelons of the party, however, there is what can only be described as a kind of Euro-fanaticism. Both Shirley Williams and David

Owen have said that they would quit the SDP if its members voted to turn it into an anti-EEC party. As we have already seen, it was opposition to the anti-EEC stance of the Labour Party in the early 1970s that brought the 'Gang of Four' together and forged the alliances that culminated in the launching of the new party ten years later. Of the ten original Social Democrat MPs who sat in the 1970 Parliament as Labour members, only one, John Horam, did not defy a three-line whip and vote with the Conservatives on the crucial vote in October 1971 in favour of the principle of entry into the EEC. Others who took part in that rebellion as Labour MPs are David Marquand, Dick Taverne and Michael Barnes, all now leading figures in the SDP. The Camden branch of the new party has the director of the European Movement, Ernest Wistrich, as its publicity supremo, while the Kensington and Chelsea branch has the founder of the Labour Committee for Europe, Norman Hart, as its co-ordinator. Every other prominent Social Democrat one meets seems to carry the battle scars of the 1975 referendum campaign.

The foreign policy of the SDP is, in fact, the most straightforward part of its programme. To Europe and NATO has only to be added a genuine, if rather vague, commitment to helping the Third World, largely through the implementation of the proposals of the Brandt Report. There is little else to say about this area of policy.

There is another policy commitment that comes across very clearly in both the statements and the books mentioned above. It is the whole area of constitutional reform. Once again, it is not a particularly novel programme, having long been advocated by the Liberals and others. At the top of the list is proportional representation, followed by more open government, with a Freedom of Information Bill, greater Parliamentary control over the Civil Service, the strengthening of Select committees and state financing of political parties, as on the Continent, to reduce their dependence on particular corporate interests.

That much is reasonably plain sailing. When it comes to the central area of economic and social policy, however, it is rather more difficult to establish exactly what the SDP stands for. Its pronouncements reveal a blend of a fairly traditional Croslandite commitment to an expanding welfare state financed through growth in a mixed economy and newer, more radical notions of market socialism, community care and decentralisation.

It is not even entirely clear whether the new party sees itself as socialist or not. Roy Jenkins maintains that it is not, and says, 'I certainly wouldn't want a party that stresses socialism.' Both David Owen and Shirley Williams, however, emphasise in their books that they are socialists and have subsequently insisted that they have not forsaken that position in joining the SDP. In *Face the Future* Owen's first chapter is entitled 'The Values of Socialism' and expresses his particular commitment to what he sees as a decentralist socialist tradition which started with guild socialism and is now represented by European social democracy. In *Politics is for People* Shirley Williams's first chapter, 'The Achievement', similarly describes her own attachment to Christian Socialism.

For those Social Democrats who do believe in it, what does socialism mean? The answer is first and foremost an overriding commitment to the pursuit of equality. The word 'socialism' may not occur in the SDP's first two statements of policy, but the word 'equality' appears a number of times, albeit with occasional qualifications. The two books are considerably more emphatic on the subject. Owen entitles his section on economic policy 'The Pursuit of Equality' and writes:

For all socialists, whether they use the label social democrat, democratic socialist or whatever position they may occupy in the political spectrum of socialism, there is common ground in one particular set of beliefs, the need to redress poverty and to reduce inequality.[5]

Shirley Williams's commitment to equality is, if anything, even greater. It leads her, for example, to advocate the abolition of public schools. This is a policy on which she is out of step with the rest of the 'Gang of Four', who see it as too great an infringement of individual liberty. But there is no doubt that for all of them, with the possible exception of Jenkins, the pursuit of equality in general comes before the pursuit of liberty. In this key respect the Social Democrats are socialists rather than liberals. Indeed, Mrs Williams made this point very clearly in her reply to David Steel's open letter to the 'Gang', published in the *Guardian* on 8 August, when she pointed out

that the stress which she, in common with other social democrats, put on equality would not be shared by many Liberals.

But if the socialism espoused by the founders of the SDP
involves them in pursuing equality, it most emphatically does
not commit them to pursuing public ownership. That, indeed,
is the subject on which the social democrats part company
from other kinds of socialist and carve out their own
distinctive position. The point is most clearly made by David
Marquand in a lecture he gave early in 1980:

It is humbug to pretend that clause-four socialists and defenders of
the mixed economy are in some mysterious way on the same side.
They are on different sides of the deepest gulf in present-day British
politics; and the only honest course is to recognise the fact by
applying different labels to them. The defenders of the mixed
economy happen to be closer to central European social democracy,
and in particular to Austrian and West German social democracy,
than to any other political tendency in the modern world. For all
these reasons, it seems to me appropriate, even if not strictly accurate
historically, to describe them as social democrats; and it seems to me
equally appropriate that they should describe themselves as such.
The most obvious distinguishing feature of social democracy, then, is
a positive commitment to the mixed economy.[6]

In his book David Owen draws a similar distinction between
what Beatrice Webb called the 'A' socialists (anarchists) and
the 'B' socialists (bureaucrats). Owen argues that the 'Bs' have
for too long been in the ascendant in the British Labour movement. 'It was too easily assumed', he writes, 'that the achievement of a much greater degree of state ownership would of
itself spread to all citizens the power previously held by private
business.'[7] Now, he suggests, it is time to let the 'A' socialists
have their head. Shirley Williams made much the same point to
me in an interview about her book:

There are two strands of socialism muddled up. Both have a common
commitment to equality and wider ownership, but there the similarity ends. The revolutionary strand is destroyed by the fact that it is
never able to answer the problem of the unchangeability of the
power it throws up. The distribution of power is as important as the
distribution of wealth and property. It seems to me that only reformist socialism can do that, and I now feel the only way is through
a pluralist economy.

The concept of the mixed economy holds a central place in the political philosophy of the Social Democrats. They see it as lying at the heart of European social democracy and as being seriously under threat both from Benn on the left and from Thatcher on the right. Once again, there is nothing very radical or new about their belief in the importance of a mix of publicly and privately owned industries, with the selective involvement of the state in the economy in both formal and informal ways. It is essentially the Butskellite creed as accepted by successive Labour and Conservative Governments from 1945 to 1979 and, some might say, as practised even by the present Government. It is also the belief of a large part of the present Labour Party. Denis Healey, for example, in a speech to the Post Office Engineering Union in May 1981, extolled the virtues of the mixed economy and praised the achievements of Austria and Norway in that area in a way which must have gladdened the hearts of any social democrats in the audience.

In more specific matters of economic policy, such as the question of what it would do about the all-important problems of inflation and unemployment, the SDP has had rather less to say. That is partly because of considerable differences of opinion on the subject within its own ranks. In a seminar at York University at the end of April, David Marquand admitted that differences over economic policy were greater than had been foreseen when the party was formed, and he pointed specifically to the contrast between Mrs Williams, who argued in favour of maximising employment even if it meant sacrificing efficiency, and John Horam, who was much more market-orientated and closer to Mrs Thatcher.

The SDP is clear about what it rejects – both the monetarism of the present Conservative administration and the Bennite alternative economic strategy of planning agreements, import controls and more nationalisation – but less clear about what it wants in their place. The natural corollary of all that it says on the subject of inflation would be support for an incomes policy, but it has fought shy of committing itself too firmly to that particular principle. The joint statement which it issued with the Liberals in June was vague on the subject, talking only of the need for 'a spirit of co-operation, which alone can provide the background for an agreed strategy for incomes'. In her book Shirley Williams opts for a voluntary policy with room for local bargaining, while David Owen advocates 'a decentralised policy that relies on a mixture of market forces, controls and comparability.[8] It seems certain that support for an incomes policy of some kind will find its way into the SDP manifesto.

On unemployment, the SDP's policy is spelt out clearly in the fourth of the 'Twelve Tasks' printed at the beginning of this chapter. It is a fairly conventional approach, which borrows heavily from the successful West German practice of providing apprenticeships for the great majority of school-leavers. However, a rather more radical approach is adopted by Mrs Williams in her book, where she argues that ultimately unemployment can be combated only by a major change of attitude on the part of manufacturers, designers and economists towards the two factors of labour and capital. 'The West has operated on the principle that you improve matters by substituting capital for labour wherever possible,' she says, 'I think we will now have to alter this whole approach.' She feels that the high and increasing costs of energy will encourage the redesign of manufacturing processes to allow for a greater input of labour. One specific proposal she makes is that instead of building a new nuclear power station, the Government should embark on a massive programme for the insulation of houses, factories and offices. The two projects would have much the same effect – the first creating energy, the second saving it – but the second would be much more labour-intensive.

That is perhaps the nearest Mrs Williams gets to the 'quantum jump' in thinking which she promises at the beginning of her book. For the most part, she and other Social Democrats see the solution to unemployment as lying primarily in the creation of conventional jobs in the formal sector of the economy as a result of economic growth. In taking this approach, the SDP appears to align itself with the Conservatives, Labour and much of the Liberal Party, and in opposition to those in the Ecology Party and other advocates of the post-industrial economy, who argue that full employment in the conventional sense will never be achieved again; that the important sector on which to concentrate is the informal or hidden economy or odd jobs, moonlighting, bartering and self-sufficiency; and that a zero rate of economic growth is both inevitable and positively advantageous. The Ecology Party, in fact, undertook an amusing exercise in which it compared the policy statements in the Limehouse Declaration with those of recent Labour, Conservative and Liberal manifestos. They were all remarkably similar – the Ecologists called the phenomenon 'the recycling of politics'.

None of the leading Social Democrats has much time for this alternative approach to Britain's economic future. In her book Mrs Williams commits herself to the traditional Keynesian goal of full employment and maintains a puritanical socialist distaste for the informal economy. Dr Owen at least nods in the direction of the no-growth lobby, but makes it clear that he thinks it is misguided:

There is a very genuine and probably growing opinion that Britain should adopt a low-growth strategy, create a low-energy society, resist the employment and social implications of the new technology, sustain old industries, refuse robots, keep the conventional office, return to the land and dismantle the industrial society. It is easy to scoff at these ideas, but they have appeal because of the despair felt at the consequences of present policies. For people to be persuaded to reject such a strategy, as not just backward-looking but as a counsel of despair that will itself bring more misery than happiness, they must be able to relate to a future where there is the prospect of a society which they control and where they do not feel the slaves of that society.[9]

The principle of decentralisation, introduced in that last extract, is almost as important an article of faith as the mixed economy to the founding fathers of the SDP. It is made much of in their first two policy statements. It runs through both David Owen's book, the second chapter of which is entitled 'the Decentralist Tradition', and Shirley Williams's. It is the theme of Lord Young's *Bigness is the Enemy of Humanity*,[10] the first of a series of policy papers produced by the party under the general title *Open Forum*.

The genesis of this commitment to decentralisation is an interesting one. In part, it is a response to the 'small is beautiful' philosophy of the 1970s and an assimilation of the prevailing anti-corporatism that has inspired both Margaret Thatcher and Tony Benn. A more specific process of rethinking has also been going on in the last two or three years among some of the leading social democrat intellectuals in Britain. Traditionally, social democracy in this country has been corporatist, centralist and identified with a high degree of state control over people's lives. Towards the end of the 1970s, under the impact of the changing economic and intellectual climate, a number of people began to question this traditional view and to revise the social democratic philosophy in a way that was even more radical than Anthony Crosland's revision of socialism had been twenty years earlier.

The first contribution to this revision was probably Evan Luard's book, *Socialism Without the State*,[11] published in the autumn of 1979. Luard, now a leading member of the SDP, is an academic who was Labour MP for Oxford from 1966 to 1970 and 1974 to 1979. The purpose of his book was simple – to strip socialism of its association with state control. In fact, he argued, that was a modern heresy. Early socialists had been concerned primarily with liberation from the state. He suggested that concentrating the means of production and sources of income and wealth in the hands of the state had positively hindered the achievement of socialism, and he called for a new, community-based approach.

Luard later expanded this idea in a Fabian pamphlet, *Socialism at the Grassroots*, published in April 1980. The Labour Party, he wrote, was preoccupied with macro-socialism (the organisation of state power) and not interested enough in micro-socialism (the rooting of socialism in the living community within which ordinary people live and work). He argued specifically for the replacement of the capitalist system of organising industry by one based on worker co-operatives; the establishment of a new pattern of regional government with directly elected regional assemblies, district councils and community councils; and the provision of help and encouragement for non-official community organisations.

The second major contribution to the development of decentralised social democracy was the lecture entitled 'Taming Leviathan', from which an extract has been quoted above, which was delivered by David Marquand in February 1980. The lecture reflected thoughts which Marquand had first developed in discussions with a group of leading thinkers from all political parties who had been brought together in the autumn of 1979 by Stan Windass, a leading proponent of the so-called 'alternative society'. The group included Lord Boyle, the former Conservative Education Minister, Jo Grimond, Dick Taverne, Professor James Meade, and Professor Ralf Dahrendorf, Director of the London School of Economics. All were agreed that the social democratic consensus which had effectively ruled Britain since the war had now broken down and that there was a need to find a new consensus.

In his lecture, Marquand argued that the overwhelming reason for the collapse of the old consensus was that

the policies through which post-war social democracy has sought to realise its fourfold commitment to personal freedom, social justice, resource redistribution and economic growth have rested, in practice, on a number of over-optimistic assumptions about the nature of the state, about the possibility of changing society by acting through the state and about the risks involved in trying to act through the state.[12]

As a result, social democracy had become a system of social engineering rather than a movement for personal liberation. It had created a new Leviathan as formidable as the all-powerful sovereign imagined by Hobbes in the mid-seventeenth century. Just as Hobbes saw his Leviathan as the only alternative to civil war, so social democrats had seen the centralised corporate state as the only alternative to social injustice.

How could this new Leviathan be tamed? In his lecture Marquand admitted that he was not entirely certain, but he offered two distinct approaches: constitutional reform along the familiar lines of proportional representation, more open government and more control over the executive, and economic decentralisation.

The first prong of a decentralist strategy must be to bypass Leviathan by strengthening the micro-economy at the expense of the macro-economy, by encouraging the forces which are already leading people to vote with their feet in favour of the micro-economy. In practice, this means helping small firms, encouraging self-employment, and making it easier to undertake local initiatives of all kinds. Above all, it means fostering what is sometimes called 'market socialism' – a state of affairs in which the workers share in the control of their enterprises, and share proportionately in the profits or losses.[13]

Following Luard's and Marquand's lead, several other prominent social democrats began to develop similar decentralist perspectives some time before the birth of the SDP. John Horam became interested in the concept of 'market socialism'. Early in 1980 Shirley Williams delivered a lecture with the 'small is beautiful' theme at the launching of an appeal for a Schumacher Centre in Britain. Both her book and David Owen's (written, of course, while they were still members of the Labour Party) repeat this message.

In terms of industrial policy, this commitment to decentralisation means support for small businesses, co-operatives and schemes for worker participation, with decision-taking brought down to the level of the shop floor. In the administrative sphere, it leads to a call for devolution, entailing a reduction in the powers of the Civil Service and an increase in those of local authorities. In his book Owen calls for elected regional assemblies, a decentralised health service in which elected local health authorities would have the power to raise their own revenue, and a system of local income tax, along the lines suggested in the Layfield Report, in order to reinvigorate local government. These last two innovations are also advocated in Lord Young's *Open Forum* pamphlet *Bigness is the Enemy of Humanity*, which additionally calls for decentralisation in education, with school governors having more power and parents more say in the running of schools, and in housing, with more tenant involvement and management by co-operatives and voluntary associations. Lord Young argues that the SDP should be determined to make local authorities something more than agents of central government and ends with the eloquent statement:

To act small is to think big. A painter is judged by the voids he leaves between the figures in his pictures; a poet by the silences between his words; the new politician will be judged by the space he leaves between central and local government.[14]

The concept of decentralisation also dominates the SDP's policy on social welfare. This is a critical area for Social Democrats. If British social democracy, as practised since the war, has an institutional embodiment, it is surely the welfare state, based on the principle of equality, financed through redistributive taxation and aiming to provide ever higher standards of comfort and care for the population as a whole. The leaders of the new party have made clear their strong commitment to the basic principle of the welfare state. Indeed, both David Owen and Shirley Williams begin their books with tributes to its creation and development over the last forty years, which they see as the crowning achievement of social democracy. Yet they have also faced up to the fact that the sustained economic growth which made possible that achievement is no longer a feature of British society, and that in the eyes of many the state has taken over from welfare, and bureaucracy has triumphed at the expense of care.

Their solution to this dilemma is to invoke the fashionable notion of greater community involvement and voluntary activity. Owen entitles his chapter on the health service 'Community Care', while Williams subtitles hers on the social services 'Involving People.' Both argue for a more community-based, devolved system for providing care, which stresses self-help and local voluntary initiatives – a welfare society, perhaps, instead of a welfare state.

There is a fundamental problem with this decentralist approach which the SDP – in common, it might be said, with many others who preach it – has yet to resolve. By its very nature, it would remove decision-making and influence from Westminster and the sphere of national politics and would put them into the hands of small local communities. Yet the SDP sees itself first and foremost as a national political party whose main objective is to win a majority in the House of Commons and to form a Government. How far would a Social Democratic Government actually live by its principles and surrender much of its power and influence? How, indeed, would it set about achieving its aim of a decentralised society? Surely that will happen, if it is going to happen at all, largely in a spontaneous and haphazard way, as a result of local initiatives and developments and not as a result of anything a Government does. The real creators of the new society, I venture to think, will be community workers, teachers, doctors, priests and others working on a small and modest scale in their own immediate environments, and not national politicians, Social Democrat or otherwise.

Apart from this general problem, there are also specific contradictions inherent in the Social Democrats' position as it has been outlined in this chapter. The greatest is that between their belief in decentralisation and their commitment to equality. The inevitable effect of decentralising government and welfare services is to increase inequalities in society. It is not difficult to see, for example, that a local health service financed and run entirely by the county of Sussex would be very different from that provided in Tyne and Wear. Some of the policies advocated by SDP leaders do, in fact, demand a high degree of intervention and control by the central state, like Shirley Williams's commitment to abolishing public schools in the interest of providing greater equality of opportunity.

The idea of an incomes policy is perhaps the prime example of a scheme in which centralism and corporatism are necessary to ensure fairness and equality of treatment. Incomes policies have worked in Britain in the past only because Governments have been prepared to surrender a substantial part of the business of governing to corporate interests, primarily the trade unions. They work in other parts of Europe, like West Germany, because of a similarly corporatist and centralised approach to pay bargaining.

The leaders of the SDP are aware of these problems and contradictions in their policies. They accept that there will always be a need for some intervention by central government but argue that it should be of a rather different kind from hitherto. Shirley Williams says:

I think that to a much greater extent than at present Government ought to set a broad framework and then let people operate freely within it. On industrial democracy, for example, it should require firms and unions to submit their own schemes which conform to broad Government outlines.

We are much too governessy at the moment. I don't think it's the business of the state to say that every woman should have her baby in hospital, although it can point out the dangers of home births. In the welfare field, I think the state should set minimum standards, supported by subsidy. Beyond that it should be up to communities to provide more, using local income tax to do so.

It is unfair to dwell too much on the inconsistencies of the SDP's policies. There are blatant contradictions in the outlook and actions of all political parties. The present Conservative Government, for example, combines an overall commitment to the principle of non-intervention and *laissez-faire* with substantial subsidies for certain industries. The Labour left manages somehow to reconcile the principle of internationalism with support for import controls and a siege economy. In this respect, indeed, the SDP may well prove better than most.

Nor is it necessarily a bad thing that much of what the Social Democrats stand for is not, in fact, quite as shining and new and radical as it might at first sight appear. The business of breaking down the centralised corporate state while at the same time combating poverty and inequality is going to be very difficult; the task is likely to be achieved through steady, almost piecemeal application rather than through brash and simple sloganizing. The accumulated débris of past Royal Commission Reports on constitutional and industrial reform, from which the SDP is now gleaning many of its policies, is not without value simply because past Governments have chosen to ignore the recommendations it contains and to retain the old systems. There is much to be said for rescuing such half-forgotten names as Maud, Kilbrandon, Layfield and Bullock from the dustbins of Whitehall.

The utterances of the leading lights of the SDP may not, on close examination, be as radical or as exciting as those of Mrs Thatcher or Mr Benn, but they may well stand more chance of being implemented. Social democracy is not a messianic creed that promises to change the world but rather an approach to the besetting problems of politics which stresses reason rather than revolution and the hard slog rather than the instant solution. It is interesting that both David Owen and Shirley Williams define it in those terms in their books. Mrs. Williams first:

The commitment to persuasion is of the essence of social democracy, and distinguishes it from other heirs to the socialist tradition. The commitment, of course, was long ago transformed into a lasting relationship between democratic socialists and the electorate, a relationship which has been an important influence on the development of socialist thought. It has modified socialist doctrine because socialist doctrine has had to be acceptable to the electorate. It has created the politics of gradualism; and it has also meant that social-ism can only advance intermittently and will sometimes suffer set-backs.[15]

Owen quotes the words of Leszek Kolakowski, a Polish-born philosopher who is now teaching at Oxford University, as the best working definition of social democracy:

The trouble with the social democratic idea is that it does not stock and does not sell any of the exciting ideological commodities which various totalitarian movements – Communists, fascists or leftists – offer dream-hungry youth. It has no ultimate solution for all human misery and misfortunes. It has no prescription for the total salvation of mankind. It cannot promise the firework of the last revolution to settle definitely all conflicts and struggles. It invented no miraculous devices to bring about the perfect unity of man and universal brotherhood. It believes in no final victory over evil. . . . It is an obstinate will to erode by inches the conditions which produce avoidable suffering, oppression, hunger, wars, racial and national hatred, insatiable greed and vindictive envy.[16]

Social democracy, then, is less an ideology and more a particular approach to dealing with society and its problems. It is an approach that has worked rather well in Europe, particularly in West Germany and Scandinavia, where it has helped to produce societies which are more prosperous, less class-ridden and perhaps also more fraternal than our own. If we ask what a Social Democratic Britain would be like, we will find an answer by looking at those countries. It would have proportional representation, state funding of political parties and possibly a federal system of government. There would be more worker participation in industry, some kind of annual agreement on incomes and more small businesses and co-operatives. Our schools and hospitals would be more autonomous and more open institutions. Above all, perhaps, our perspective would be less insular and more enthusiastically European and internationalist.

At first sight, it may seem unlikely that the chauvinist and conservative British electorate will vote for a party which wants to model the country on this Continental pattern. Will it not prefer the John Bullish nationalism of Foot and Benn on the one side or Thatcher and Whitelaw on the other to the

internationalism and pro-Europeanism of the 'Gang of Four'?
Perhaps. But it is also quite possible that as they contemplate
Britain's decline, the voters may agree with the Social Democrats that it is worth taking a few tips from those countries
which are still managing to flourish.

*'It's very convenient, you can join by credit card and at the same
time write everything they stand for on the back of it.'*
(Guardian, *27 March 1981*)

CHAPTER 8

Breaking the Mould?
The performance and prospects of the SDP

Political forecasting is a difficult business at the best of times. Trying to predict the outcome of an election held under the British first-past-the-post system between three political groupings with roughly equal levels of support is well-nigh impossible. Yet that is what this chapter must try to do, since the opinion polls suggest that this will be the most likely scenario for the next General Election in or before 1984. That election could well determine the fate of the SDP. First, however, it is worth reviewing the evidence that is already available on the performance and prospects of the party, which may help in an assessment of whether it is, indeed, likely to achieve its bold aim of breaking the mould of British politics.

At this early stage of its development, does the SDP look as if it will climb into the same league as the Conservative, Labour and Liberal parties, or is it more likely to join those peripheral and short-lived groupings like the Liberal Unionists and Mosley's New Party? The first thing to be said is that it starts with a more substantial base and in a more auspicious electoral climate than any other breakaway group since the Labour Party was formed at the beginning of this century. With fifteen MPs, following the defection from the Labour Party in July of James Wellbeloved, a former junior minister and Opposition Whip, the SDP has a larger representation in Parliament than any third party since 1935. It seems almost certain that there will be more Social Democrats in the Commons by the time of the next General Election as a result of further defections from Labour and of by-election victories.

The party's membership too is already considerably greater than that of any previous breakaway party. Although the figure of 51,849 members recruited in the first eight weeks after the launch may seem small beer compared to the one million or so members claimed by the Conservatives, the 350,000 by Labour and the 180,000 by the Liberals, it represents a considerable achievement and puts the party well on target for its aim of having 100 members in each constituency (i.e., 63,500 altogether) by the end of 1981. Furthermore, it seems likely that because the party is new, and because of the way in which it has so far recruited, the SDP will have a much higher proportion of active and highly motivated workers among its members and fewer 'passengers' than the other parties.

Admittedly, in terms of finance and organisation it still looks a long way from being in the same league as Labour and the Conservatives. Although the £20,000-a-year salary which it is paying its chief executive is reputedly more than that received by the General Secretary of the Labour Party, the £750,000 which the SDP reckons to spend in the financial year 1981–2 is only a quarter of the budgets of the two major parties. However, the amount of free advertising which the party is receiving from the media by virtue of its novelty must to a certain extent compensate for this, just as the enthusiasm of its volunteer helpers makes up for its lack of paid staff.

Both the Liberal and Labour parties benefited in their early days from an extension of the franchise, which gave them the votes of a brand-new electorate. Short of the unlikely eventuality for the vote being granted to 15-year-olds, the SDP is not going to be helped in this way. However, as has already been pointed out in chapters 5 and 6, there are good grounds for supposing that the party will have a strong appeal for the new electorate that has emerged over the last twenty or so years as a result of Britain's transformation from a predominantly industrial to a service-based economy. The professional and technical workers who are in the van of this post-industrial revolution form a new constituency which is free of the old ties of class and occupation that formerly linked voters with either Labour or the Conservatives.

There are other social factors which should help the SDP. As we have seen, the British electorate became far more volatile in the 1970s and much less wedded to the two-party system. Although the results of the 1979 election appeared to reverse this trend, it seems likely that it will persist through the 1980s. Certainly, the traditional class basis of political loyalty seems likely to become progressively less dominant. One of its strongest components, the manual working-class vote which is 'solid' for Labour, will steadily diminish as fewer and fewer people are employed in manufacturing and other manual occupations. As the proletariat gradually disappears, so also may the party which was partly its creation.

There are also signs of a change in the intellectual mood of the nation which is comparable with the wave of liberal optimism which accompanied the birth of the Liberal Party and the new spirit of collectivism which heralded the birth of Labour. This time the change is manifest in a revolt against corporatism and centralisation, a feeling that 'small is beautiful' and that there are no grand and simple solutions to the country's besetting problems. As yet, this new mood of political modesty and humility is confined largely to the middle classes, and it will be some time before it percolates through to the nation as a whole. But that it exists cannot be denied, and if the Social Democrats are to catch this new tide and to follow in the wake of the Liberal and Labour parties, they must reckon with the possibility that it could be twenty years before they became a fully established party.

Turning from these rather theoretical speculations to the somewhat more concrete findings of the opinion polls, there is strong evidence that, at least in its first few months of existence, the SDP has managed to attract the support of a substantial proportion of the electorate. The four Gallup polls conducted for the *Daily Telegraph* in the three months following the party's launch show support for a SDP/Liberal alliance running at an average of 42.6 per cent and consistently exceeding support for either of the two main existing parties (see table 3). Admittedly, they also show that support for an alliance has dropped steadily since the SDP was launched, but in general pollsters say that they are surprised how well the party has continued to perform at a time when the initial euphoria of the launch has worn off and it has to some extent lost the attention of the media.

At first sight, the findings of the four MORI polls conducted in the same period, and also reproduced in table 3, present a more

TABLE 3: THE SDP's PERCENTAGE RATING IN OPINION POLLS, END MARCH TO END JUNE 1981

Gallup polls for Daily Telegraph

	2 April[1]			16 April[2]			14 May[3]			18 June[4]		
Conservative	30	25.5	n/a	30	25	25.5	32	28	28.5	29.5	28	27.5
Labour	30.5	24.5	n/a	34.5	29	28	35.5	29.5	28.5	37.5	33.5	33.5
Liberal	18	12		14	12		18	14		18	14.5	
SDP	19	36		19	32.5		11	25.5		12.5	23	
SDP–Liberal alliance			48.5			45			40			37

MORI polls for New Standard and Sunday Times

	—[5]			5 May[6]			14 June[7]			2 July[8]		
Conservative	28	24	n/a	30	28	30	35	29	33	31	n/a	27
Labour	38	30	n/a	38	33	35	39	33	35	39	n/a	32
Liberal	17	14	n/a	17	14	n/a	14	11	n/a	16	n/a	n/a
SDP	15	29	n/a	12	23	n/a	10	24	n/a	12	n/a	n/a
SDP–Liberal alliance			n/a			29			30			39

[1]Fieldwork 25–31 March.
[2]Fieldwork 8–13 April.
[3]Fieldwork 6–11 May.
[4]Fieldwork 9–15 June.
[5]Unpublished; fieldwork 19–23 March.
[6]Fieldwork 23–9 April.
[7]Fieldwork 29–30 May.
[8]Fieldwork 18–22 June.

Note: In each poll the first column shows answers to the standard unprompted question: 'How would you vote in a General Election tomorrow?' The second column shows answers to a prompted question reminding respondents of the existence of the SDP. The third column shows answers to a question suggesting a SDP–Liberal alliance.

confusing picture. This is largely because MORI twice changed the questions which it asked. In the first poll, at the end of March, people were simple asked the standard unprompted question about how they would vote in a General Election tomorrow and a second, similar question which reminded them of the existence of the SDP. In the next two polls, in April and May, they were asked an additional question which raised the possibility of a SDP/Liberal alliance but asked specifically how they would vote if the Liberals stood down in favour of the SDP in their constituency. This way of putting the question may well account for the discrepancy between the 29 to 30 per cent support for the alliance suggested by MORI and the 40 per cent noted by Gallup, who asked a much simpler question. In their June poll MORI changed their question to one much more like Gallup's ('If the SDP and the Liberals formed an alliance at the next election, which party would you vote for?') and obtained a very similar result.

Opinion polls, of course, are not necessarily reliable guides to how people would actually vote in an election. Particularly when they are taken in the middle of a Government's term of office and when they involve prompted questions, both of which apply to the polls reproduced in table 3, they tend to exaggerate the degree of support that minor parties would actually receive in a General Election. Polls taken after the Orpington by-election in 1962 showed that the Liberals had more support than either of the two parties and even, in some cases, the backing of more than 50 per cent of the electorate. Yet in the General Election two years later the party polled only 11.2 per cent of the vote.

Having entered this strong caveat, however, it is still worth examining the findings of the polls because they furnish important evidence about the nature of support for the SDP, even if they are less reliable indicators of the possible extent of that support in a General Election. One point is immediately obvious from a glance at the figures in table 3. It is that support for the new party effectively doubles when people are reminded of its existence (answers in the second column of each poll) as distinct from being asked the standard unprompted question about how they would vote in a General Election tomorrow (the first column). There is nothing unusual in this, of course.

Prompted questions always produce a reply which is more favourable to the commodity mentioned than unprompted ones. But the degree of discrepancy in this case suggests that the SDP has a credibility problem. Three months after its launch, and following enormous coverage in the media, it has still not impressed itself on the minds of many electors as a party which they can and will vote for at the next election. They need to be reminded of its existence before they say they will support it. Admittedly, this problem is likely to diminish as the party becomes better established and as it puts up candidates in by-elections, but it may take some considerable time to disappear. The British electorate is not renowned for its deep knowledge of politics.

The two polls reproduced in table 3 conflict on the question of whether support for a SDP/Liberal alliance is apparently greater than the combined level of support for the two parties if they stand separately. Gallup suggests that it is; MORI, however, indicates that there would be significant defections from both parties if they formed an alliance. The discrepancy may result in part from the way in which MORI phrased its question: 'If a new Social Democratic Party made an alliance with the Liberal Party, and the Liberals decided not to stand in this constituency, then which party would you vote for?' Other MORI polls suggest that fewer people would support a Liberal alliance candidate than a SDP alliance candidate. They also suggest that whereas 65 per cent of SDP supporters would back a Liberal candidate standing on an alliance ticket, only 50 per cent of Liberals would vote for a SDP candidate in similar circumstances. These findings suggest that in practice the alliance might well have less support than is evident from the answers to Gallup's more general question.

More detailed poll findings provide an interesting geographical breakdown of the SDP's support. In general, they show that while it is spread more evenly across the country than support for either Labour or the Conservatives, it is stronger in the South than in the North. In answer to the standard unprompted question in MORI's poll at the end of May, 13 per cent of those living in the South and only 9 per cent of those in the North said they would vote SDP in the next election. However, when they were reminded of its existence, their response was much more even; 24 per cent of southerners and 23 per cent of northerners expressed their support.

Even more detailed polls, like that reproduced in table 4, suggest that support for the SDP is strongest in predominantly rural Conservative areas, such as the South-West, central Southern and South-East England and East Anglia, and weakest in the traditional Labour heartlands of Scotland and the North-East. Individual polls conducted in particular constituencies tend to confirm that the new party has failed to make significant headway in industrial areas with a strong Labour tradition. At the end of January, for example, MORI conducted a poll for Granada Television in the constituencies of the eleven Labour MPs who had so far joined the Council for Social Democracy. All but three of these constituencies were in industrial areas in the northern half of England. The poll found that if the eleven stood as social democrats, they would receive the support of 32 per cent of their electors, with 39 per cent supporting Labour candidates. A poll conducted by MORI for the *Sunday Times* in April in Bill Rodgers's Stockton-on-Tees constituency found that 34 per cent would vote for him as a Social Democrat, while 48 per cent would back a rival Labour candidate. Of the original fourteen SDP MPs, only David Owen (Plymouth, Devonport), Robert Maclennan (Caithness and Sutherland) and Christopher Brocklebank-Fowler (North-West Norfolk) would have a good chance of holding their present seats in a General Election if the party's apparent poor showing in traditional Labour areas were maintained.

The SDP's regional breakdown of its own membership at the end of April revealed a similar pattern of support. More than half of its first 50,000 members were concentrated in the four regions of Greater London, East Anglia, the South and Wessex, and the South-East. Membership was lowest in Scotland, Wales and the North-East. It is also noticeable that there have been very few defections to the Social Democrats among Labour councillors in the major industrial conurbations. A survey which I carried out for *The Times* at the end of May of the ten largest metropolitan district councils (Birmingham, Leeds, Sheffield, Liverpool, Manchester, Bradford, Kirklees, Coventry, Wigan and Wirral) indicated that there had not been

TABLE 4 REGIONAL BREAKDOWN OF PERCENTAGE SUPPORT FOR SDP–LIBERAL ALLIANCE, END OF APRIL 1981

	Scotland %	North-East %	Lancs %	Yorks %	Midlands %	Wales & West %	East Anglia %	London %	South[1] %	South-West %
Conservative	19	32	27	25	35	26	39	31	34	30
Labour	38	39	43	44	32	40	19	39	24	23
SDP-Liberal	23	23	26	28	30	30	36	25	39	42

[1]The South television area includes both central southern and south-eastern England.

Source: MORI poll for *New Standard*, fieldwork undertaken between 23 and 27 April.

Note: Regions are Independent Television areas. Answers are to a question asking 'If a new Social Democratic Party made an alliance with the Liberal Party, and the Liberals decided not to stand in this constituency, then which party would you vote for?'

a single defection to the SDP. In the ten largest non-metropolitan district councils, three Labour councillors had defected, significantly all in the South (two in Bristol and one in Plymouth).

Another more impressionistic piece of evidence confirms the party's failure as yet to make much impression on the traditional Labour strongholds. When, in the wake of the Limehouse Declaration, *The Times* sent reporters out and about to gauge support for a new social democrat party they found considerable enthusiasm in the Home Counties and the South, but scepticism in the North-East and in the more marginal West Midlands. The difference between North and South in terms of the response of working-class people was epitomised in the contrasting comments of a retired railway worker in Newcastle ('I can tell you, any sort of centre party is a waste of time and money here') and a retired delivery driver in Southampton who was determined to support the social democrats ('All the others are Marxists. The true Labour crowd are breaking away. The sooner they go in with Steel and form a good, solid party, the sooner we will get rid of Maggie').[1]

There is another message from the polls that should cause some worry at Queen Anne's Gate. Although those who say they will support the SDP seem to be in general agreement with its overall policies, there is one important issue, Britain's continued membership of the EEC, on which they oppose the party's stance. Furthermore, there is a general lack of awareness, even among supporters, of what the SDP stands for and a much more tenuous identification with it than is the case with supporters of other parties.

This fact was clear from the MORI poll conducted at the end of April. Those who said they would vote for the SDP were shown a number of policies and asked, first, whether they thought the SDP would support or oppose them and, second, what their own views were. The results, in percentages, are shown overleaf.

Given the lack of unity within the SDP over some of those policies, it is perhaps a remarkable tribute to the perspicacity of the British public that a majority of them have correctly identified the party's policy in every case. Nor is it surprising that on an issue like the abolition of public schools, over which

Policy		SDP's attitude			Supporters' views	
	For	Against	Don't know	For	Against	Don't know
Introduce proportional representation	61	11	28	55	16	29
Introduce incomes policy	59	11	30	46	23	31
Take Britain out of EEC	37	45	18	54	37	9
Unilateral disarmament	26	48	26	30	60	10
More nationalisation	19	66	15	21	70	9
Abolish public schools	34	36	30	25	67	8
Replace rates with local income tax	31	24	44	42	32	26

there is a clear conflict within the 'Gang of Four', they are uncertain about what the party's policy is. However, the poll suggests that on any one issue, between 34 and 68 per cent of SDP supporters are ignorant about where the party stands. It also suggests that on one particular issue, Britain's continued membership of the EEC, they are out of step with the party. It happens to be the issue on which the 'Gang of Four' have committed themselves most clearly and unequivocally.

The apparent incompatibility between the views of the leadership and those of the majority of potential supporters about the desirability of keeping Britain in the EEC could well damage the SDP's chances at the next election. A MORI poll for the BBC *Analysis* programme found that 58 per cent of SDP supporters would vote in a referendum to come out of the EEC and only 39 per cent would vote to stay in.[2] It seems almost certain that at the next election the Labour Party will play the anti-EEC card for all it is worth and make the most of the SDP's pro-Market stance. In doing so, it may well deter a significant proportion of those who now say that they support the SDP from actually voting for them.

The fact that almost as many of those questioned in the MORI poll thought that it was the party's policy to bring Britain out of the EEC as to keep us in points to another significant feature about the SDP. It is in many ways a wish-fulfilment party; many of its supporters see it not as what it is but as what they think it ought to be. This may be partly the result of the way the idea of a new centre party has been presented by the media as a kind of universal cure-all and generally a 'good thing'. It also probably reflects the way the SDP sold itself at its launch as a party of common sense, moderation and good men and true who were against sin and in favour of virtue. Amid the platitudes, and given the lack of hard, specific policy statements, it was easy for many voters to regard the Social Democrats as their sort of people.

This image has both its strengths and weaknesses. Clearly, the more the people who think the party stands for what they themselves favour, regardless of whether it does or not, the more votes the SDP will get. But there is obviously also a terrible danger of disillusionment. The voter who backs the SDP because he thinks it will take him out of the EEC is in for a shock. So is the Birmingham butcher who told a *Times* reporter that he would vote for the SDP if it supported enforced conscription for the unemployed and the return of hanging.[3]

The corollary of meaning all things to all men is that you don't mean very much to any of them. A Gallup poll in February found that only 17.8 per cent of potential supporters for a new social democratic party said they felt a close sense of identification with it, compared with 31.8 per cent of Conservative supporters who identified closely with the party of their choice and 46 per cent of Labour supporters. The SDP may well inspire stronger feelings of loyalty as it builds up its local organisation, but these feelings are unlikely, for some time, to become as strong as those inspired by the Conservative and Labour parties, with their clearer class and geographical identities.

Turning from ratings in the polls to actual performance in elections, at the time this book was being written there were only three pieces of evidence to hand: the showing of those who stood as Social Democrats in the May county council elections, the results of the first batch of local council by-elections contested by the SDP in July, and the result of the Warrington by-election on 16 July. Since the SDP refused to endorse any of those who stood in the county elections, it may seem unfair to take their performance as an indication of support for the party in the country. However, since in the minds of most electors the Social Democrat candidates were associated with the new party, and since they benefited from the publicity surrounding its launch, it is not unreasonable to look at the results they achieved as part of an overall survey of the amount of support the Social Democrats are likely to rally in a General Election.

Of the ninety-six candidates who stood as Social Democrats in the elections outside London, I have been able to discover six victors. Two were in Lincolnshire, which has had several democratic Labour councillors since Taverne's breakaway in 1973, and one each in Clwyd, Shropshire, Oxfordshire and East Sussex, where Tom Forester, an industrial journalist, scored a particular triumph in Brighton, polling more than 55 per cent of the vote.

In London, where the SDA mounted a concerted campaign led by Lord George-Brown in eight seats with left-wing Labour candidates, the results were poor. The Social Democrats' share of the poll ranged from 19 per cent in Islington South, where Douglas Eden stood against Frances Morrell, former political adviser to Tony Benn, to 4.5 per cent in Wandsworth, Putney. They were always in third place, although in seven of the eight seats where they stood they pushed the Liberals into fourth place. Nowhere was the combined Liberal/Social Democrat vote bigger than that of the winning party, although in two boroughs (Islington South and Walthamstow) it was bigger than that of the second party.

The first opportunity that any voters had to show their support for the SDP proper was in a district council by-election in Sedgefield, county Durham, on 2 July. At first sight, the victory obtained by the party's candidate, David Shand, in this staunchly Labour area, seemed to justify Bill Rodgers' comment that it showed the SDP was digging deeply into the industrial heartland of Britain. However, the seat was, in fact, won from the Conservatives and with no official Labour opposition.

The result of the second council by-election contested by the

SDP, also in the North East, seemed to provide more solid evidence of its ability to erode the Labour vote in an area in which it had traditionally been very strong. Jim Heads, a shipyard shop steward, won the previously safe Labour Walkergate ward on Newcastle City Council for the new party by just one vote on 16 July.

The first big test of the SDP's support among the electorate came in the parliamentary by-election in Warrington, Cheshire, which was also held on 16 July. From the Social Democrats's point of view the solidly working-class industrial town was an unfortunate seat to have to fight so early in their party's life. It was the sixtieth safest Labour seat in the country and, according to computer calculations, was the 551st most winnable seat for the new SDP/Liberal alliance.

However, the party made the best of a bad job and entered its first major election campaign with gusto. After some initial dithering by Shirley Williams about whether or not she wanted to fight the seat, Roy Jenkins gallantly stepped in and took up the standard. He fought a vigorous and enthusiastic campaign, helped by eager volunteers who came from all over the country and by such imaginative and unconventional visual aides as a mobile Punch and Judy show designed to portray the ding-dong nature of the two party system. Privately, leading members of the party hoped for a respectable second place and for around 30 to 35 per cent of the vote, a target which opinion polls conducted in the last few days of the campaign suggested was realistic.

In the event, Mr Jenkins obtained 42.4 per cent of the vote and came within 1,759 votes of defeating the victorious Labour candidate, Doug Hoyle. The Labour majority tumbled from 32.8 to 6 per cent and the Conservatives were pushed into a derisory third place, with only 7 per cent of the vote and a lost deposit. From the small Liberal base in the 1979 General Election, there had been a swing of 23.3 per cent to the SDP/Liberal alliance. Just under three quarters of those who had voted Conservative and about a quarter of those who had voted Labour in 1979 switched to the new alliance. The votes cast for the three main party candidates were as follows:

Doug Hoyle (Labour)   14,280 (48.4 per cent)

| Roy Jenkins (SDP with Liberal support) | 12,521 (42.4 per cent) |
| Stanley Sorrell (Conservative) | 2,102 (7.1 per cent) |

It was not surprising that Mr Jenkins described the result as the most sensational in any by-election since the war. A computer prediction by the BBC for the next General Election on the basis of the votes cast at Warrington gave the SDP/Liberal alliance 501 seats in the House of Commons, Labour 113 and the Conservatives only one.

It would be a mistake, however, to read too much significance into the Warrington result. By-elections generally prove much more favourable to third parties than General Elections, as the Liberals have consistently found to their cost. The vote which they achieved at Orpington in 1962, for example, would have been enough to have put them into power at a general election. Yet in the 1964 General Election they polled only 11 per cent and won their usual handful of seats. The SDP could well face the same experience.

Yet, even allowing for the freakishness of by-elections, the result at Warrington still represents an extraordinary triumph for a new political party less than four months old and fighting in extremely unpromising territory. It also strongly suggests that the opinion polls quoted earlier in this chapter may have under-rated the level of support for the SDP/Liberal alliance in the country and particularly in traditional Labour heartlands. If, as seems likely, it is followed by similar or even better results in other by-elections, the SDP will go into the next General Election with a serious chance of breaking the mould of British politics and destroying the two party system.

A crop of local government by-election victories on July 23, exactly a week after Warrington, certainly suggested that the new party was keeping up its momentum across the country. An SDP candidate polled 52 per cent of the vote to win a Labour seat on Hemel Hempstead District Council in Hertfordshire and Social Democrats and Liberals together captured three town council seats in the staunchly Conservative territory of Guisborough, Cleveland. The most spectacular result of all, almost as impressive as that in Warrington, came in the left-wing Labour stronghold of Lambeth in London. A Social Democrat and a Liberal, fighting in alliance, took two previously rock-solid Labour seats on the borough council. Repeated across the country, these results would put the SDP/Liberal alliance in a commanding position after the local government elections of May 1982.

Before looking at the likely result of the next General Election, there is one further piece of evidence which it is interesting to examine and which the Social Democrats themselves, with their strong Europeanism, would surely want to be included. That is the performance of similar breakaway groups in other countries. Their experiences have been mixed and offer only limited encouragement to the SDP.

A surprising number of breakaway parties have been formed in Europe because of a feeling that the main socialist party in certain countries was too left-wing or Communist-dominated. The oldest-established is the Italian Social Democratic Party, which split from the Socialist Party after the Second World War. Although it took half the Socialist Party's previous vote at its first General Election in 1948, its vote then dropped. It reunited with the Socialists in the 1960s and split off again at the end of the decade. In the 1979 election it took 3.8 per cent of the vote, compared with 9.8 per cent for the main Socialist Party, and, thanks to proportional representation, won twenty seats in Parliament.

In Denmark a new Centre Democrat party launched in 1972 by Erhard Jakobsen, a former Social Democrat MP who believed his party had moved too far to the left, polled only 7.9 per cent in its first election, and its vote was down to 3.2 per cent in 1979. A similar breakaway group from the Socialist Workers Party in Luxembourg polled 9 per cent in 1974 but only 6 per cent in 1979. In France a group of ten deputies who left the Parti Socialiste when it formed the Union of the Left with the Communists in 1972 fared badly in the 1978 elections with only two retaining their seats. Outside Europe similar social democrat breakaway parties have also fared badly. One started in Japan in 1952 began by beating the main left-wing party, but then reunited with it before splitting again, as occurred in Italy, and is now the weaker of the two. In Australia a Democratic Labour Party, which broke away from the Labour Party because it claimed it was close to Communism, polled 9.4 per cent of the vote in 1958 but now has negligible support.

There is one Continental party, however, whose recent experience could be regarded by the SDP as a hopeful portent. It is the D-66 party in the Netherlands, which was set up in 1966 with the explicit goal of breaking up the existing party system. In its first election in 1967 it won only 4.5 per cent of the vote, and the proportion was down to 4.2 per cent in 1972. However, in the Dutch election held in May 1981 the party was generally agreed to be the clearest winner, increasing its share of the vote to just over 11 per cent and its number of MPs to seventeen; at the time of writing, it seems almost certain that D-66 will become a partner in the new coalition Government. Yet it would be wrong to draw too many parallels between D-66 and the SDP. In policy matters, for example, the two parties are very different. D-66 takes a strong ecological line and campaigns strenuously against the stationing of American cruise missiles on Dutch soil.[4]

How well is Britain's new breakaway party likely to do in the next General Election? The answer is dependent almost entirely on what happens to the Labour and Conservative parties in the meantime. The SDP is in an extremely frustrating position: it can do virtually nothing, by itself, to improve or even to damage its electoral chances. This has been the experience of the Liberals in the last ten years or so. It is a well-known fact of British political life that many people vote against rather than for parties. This is particularly true of the growing band of floating voters. Votes which they cast for the Conservatives are often in reality votes to keep the socialists out, and those cast for Labour are often inspired by equally hostile feelings towards the Tories. When people feel fed up with both main parties, as they have done increasingly in the last ten years, they turn to others.

The SDP is therefore crucially dependent on both the Labour and Conservative parties' continuing to appear to be dominated by extremists and by unpopular leaders, as they are at the moment. If Tony Benn wins the Labour deputy leadership contest, and if the party continues to move leftwards, there are likely to be concrete gains for the SDP as a result of further defections from Labour MPs, as well as more votes at the election. If, on the other hand, Denis Healey remains deputy leader and the Solidarity campaign launched in the party after the breakaway of the 'Gang of Four' succeeds in stemming the advance of the left, the outlook will be much bleaker for the SDP.

The Conservatives' performance and image is equally critical. If they can succeed in bringing down inflation and unemployment before the election and in appearing before the electorate with both an efficient and a humane face in the 'One Nation' tradition, there is little chance that the SDP will make substantial inroads into the Tory vote. If things go badly, however, and particularly if unemployment does not fall and it continues to be easy for Mrs Thatcher to be portrayed as narrowly doctrinaire and divisive, the SDP's chances will look very much brighter.

It seems safe to assume that the SDP/Liberal alliance will do at least as well as the Liberals alone did in February 1974, when they won 19.3 per cent of the vote. Indeed, it should not be difficult for the alliance easily to better that performance. Each period of Conservative government in the last twenty years has produced a swing to the Liberals higher than the last, and there is no reason to think that Mrs Thatcher can reverse this trend. However much the Labour Party pulls itself together, it is bound to lose some of its voters to the SDP. At this stage a vote for the alliance of between 30 and 35 per cent looks a distinct possibility. The Warrington result suggests that it could well be higher.

Even if it were possible to predict with rather more accuracy each party's share of the vote at the next election, however, it would still be extremely difficult to forecast the result in terms of seats. In a contest between three roughly equal challengers, the British election system will become a lottery in which the normal rules of swing go by the board. It would be quite possible for an SDP/Liberal alliance to gain 30 per cent of the vote and not win a single seat. Even with 35 per cent, it might win only twenty or so seats. However, with 37 per cent of the vote it could become the second biggest party in Parliament, and with 39 per cent it might well be the largest party and able to form a Government. Just a few percentage points separate complete victory from total oblivion.

The SDP will go into the next election with two serious handicaps. The first is its reasonably even spread of support across the country. In an electoral system based on proportional representation this would be an asset. In the British first-past-the-post system it is a considerable liability. Both the two major parties consistently win more seats than their share of the vote strictly entitles them to because their support is disproportionately concentrated in certain parts of the country, the Conservatives in the rural and suburban South and parts of the Midlands, Labour in the cities and the industrial North and Wales. The country has actually become more polarised in this respect over the last twenty-five years, with industrial and city areas becoming more solidly Labour as their more prosperous middle-class inhabitants have increasingly migrated to the suburbs and the countryside.

The effect of this concentration is to make it very difficult for a third party with support evenly spread across the country to pick up many seats. The Liberals suffered in this way in the two elections of 1974. By contrast, smaller parties which themselves have strongly concentrated support, like the Scottish and Welsh Nationalists, do well. In the October 1974 election, for example, the two nationalist parties, with only 3.5 of the total United Kingdom vote between them, won fourteen seats, while the Liberals, with 18.3 per cent of the vote, won only thirteen.

Now although support for an SDP/Liberal alliance appears to be more evenly spread than that either of the two main parties, it does seem to be more popular in some parts of the country than in others. On the evidence of table 4 (p. 146), such an alliance is likely to do best in the South-West, the central South and the South-East, where it apparently leads the field, and in East Anglia, where it stands second to the Conservatives. It is weakest, as we have already noted, in the industrial Labour heartlands.

This state of affairs provides the SDP with its second handicap. The seats which look most winnable are in precisely those areas of the country where the Liberals are strongest and where they could be expected to be most reluctant to stand down in favour of SDP candidates. In traditional Labour areas, where the SDP might be expected to be given a relatively free run by the

Liberals, their prospects look considerably less bright. It is in those Conservative-held seats in the South and in East Anglia where the Liberals lie second at present and the new party would seem even after Warrington to have its greatest chances of success. Yet in how many of them will the incumbent Liberal candidate be prepared to stand down in favour of a SDP candidate? Some hard bargaining lies ahead.

There are other reasons why a Liberal/SDP alliance is likely to do better in Conservative seats than in Labour ones. First, Labour's support is geographically even more concentrated that than of the Tories. Within the cities and industrial conurbations there are a large number of Labour seats with enormous majorities. They are virtually impregnable to attack from any other party. The Conservatives have far fewer safe seats of this kind. Labour's strength is graphically illustrated by a computer analysis carried out at Bristol University. This suggests that if the two main parties' share of the vote dropped to only 24 per cent each, Labour would still be left with 100 seats and the Conservatives with only one. The Conservatives need 30 per cent of the vote to hold 100 seats, while a Liberal/SDP alliance would need at least 32 per cent.[5]

Second, Conservative seats are much more vulnerable to the existing third-party challenge. Of the 339 seats won by the Conservatives at the last election, the Liberals came second in seventy-nine. Of the 269 seats won by Labour, however, the Liberals were second in only two. Given the failure of the SDP to make much impression as yet on the Labour heartlands, it is impossible at this stage to avoid the conclusion that, whatever the main sources of its support and the relative share of the vote polled by the other parties, if the alliance is going to win seats at the next election, they will come predominantly from the Conservatives.

Significantly, this is the common finding of four different attempts to predict the outcome of the next election which have so far been made on the basis of a strong third-party challenge. The Bristol University computer analysis already mentioned, for example, which was carried out as a strictly impartial academic exercise, predicted that if all three groupings polled 32 per cent each, Labour would end up with 311 seats, the Conservatives with 209 and the Liberal–SDP alliance with only eighty-nine. Even if the alliance vote rose to 37 per cent and that of the two other parties dropped to 30 per cent, the analysis still found that Labour would win with 285 seats, the alliance would come second with 272 and the Conservatives third with fifty-four.

Similar sets of results have been predicted in both Liberal and Labour party publications. In a pamphlet entitled *First Past the Post: The Great British Class Handicap,* published by the Liberal Action Group for Electoral Reform in 1980, Michael Steed and David Faull concentrate simply on a three-party fight between Conservatives, Labour and Liberals. However, their analysis of the likely Liberal performance is applicable to an alliance of that party with the SDP. They suggest that if each of the three parties won 33 per cent of the vote, the outcome in English seats would be Labour 253, Conservative 207 and Liberal fifty-six. Even if the Liberal vote rose to 37.5 per cent and Labour's fell to 30.75 per cent, Labour would remain the largest party in Parliament.[6]

A prediction of the likely outcome of the next election made by Alan Taylor in the Labour Party newspaper *Labour Weekly* produced a result remarkably similar to that of the Bristol University analysis. Assuming a 10 per cent swing away from both Conservatives and Labour to the new alliance, together with a 5 per cent swing from the Conservatives to Labour, it predicted a Labour victory with 320 seats but only 31.9 per cent of the vote, the Conservatives coming second with 189 seats and 28.9 per cent of the vote and the alliance coming third with only ninety-three seats, despite winning the highest share (33.8 per cent) of the vote. On the assumption that the Liberals would stand in those seats where they came second to the Conservatives, Mr Taylor calculated that they would win eighty-seven of the alliance seats and the SDP only six.[7]

The Road from Limehouse to Westminster,[8] a psephological study by Matthew Oakeshott, the former political adviser to Roy Jenkins, offers the SDP rather more hopeful prospects. However, it contains the same underlying message, that a good vote for the alliance will principally benefit the Labour Party. Using the February 1974 General Election results as a base, Oakeshott calculates that a 4 per cent swing to an SDP/Liberal alliance from both the two main parties would lead to a

Labour victory with 295 seats (30 per cent of the vote), the Conservatives coming second with 266 seats (34 per cent) and the alliance third with fifty seats (27 per cent). A 4 per cent swing from the Conservatives and an 8 per cent swing from Labour would leave the two main parties neck and neck (the Conservatives with 255 seats and 34 per cent of the vote, Labour with 252 seats and 30 per cent) and the alliance with 103 seats and 31 per cent of the vote.

There is one important factor which these predictions fail to take into account and which is likely to make the result of the next General Election rather less favourable to Labour than they suggest. That is the effect of the redrawing of constituency boundaries which is now in progress. It is estimated that this process could lead to the loss of up to forty seats which are at present held by Labour, the majority of them in inner-city areas where the population has fallen significantly over the last few years. The new seats which will be created will be mostly in the developing suburban and semi-rural areas that are more likely to return Conservative MPs.

Although boundary changes should have a certain corrective effect, they will by no means totally eliminate the distortion and unfairness implicit in the British electoral system which the above predictions underline. A change in that system would clearly be in the interests of the SDP and the Liberals, probably on balance in the interests of the Conservatives, and certainly against the interests of the Labour Party which does best out of the first-past-the-post system. This presents the SDP with an alarming prospect. If it does well in the next election and wins a significant number of seats, it could well put into power a left-wing Labour Government which will firmly resist all demands for proportional representation. If it does less well, however, the new Conservative Government which might well be elected could prove amenable to a change in the electoral system.

The best result for the SDP–Liberal alliance, short of an outright victory, which seems extremely unlikely, would be a hung Parliament in which it held the balance between the two main parties. The alliance could then give its support to the Conservatives in return for a commitment to introduce proportional representation at the next election. Several of those close to Mrs Thatcher believe that despite her own opposition to changing the electoral system, it is a bargain she would be prepared to make if it offered her the chance of a further term in office.

A hung Parliament after the next General Election must be regarded as a distinct possibility. One of the effects of the greater geographical concentration of Labour and Conservative support has been a decrease in the number of marginal seats which regularly change hands between the parties and give them their majorities in the House of Commons. As a result of this decline, a swing in votes from one party to the other now produces far fewer transferred seats than it used to, and as a result safe Parliamentary majorities are becoming less and less common. The task for the SDP at the next election is to do well enough to produce a hung Parliament and hold the balance, but not so well that it gives Labour an overall majority.[9]

The situation is a mass of paradoxes. If the SDP does well at the next election, it will almost certainly help the party which it has broken away from and may diminish the chances of effecting the change in the electoral system that it needs if it is to establish itself as a major and enduring feature of the British political scene. The effect of its arrival may well be to help the Liberals, some of whom wanted to strangle it at birth, to achieve the breakthrough they have so long sought. It is not difficult to imagine after the next election a victorious alliance contingent of MPs which consists of only a handful of Social Democrats, perhaps just three or four of the existing MPs, and a substantial number – perhaps fifty or more – of Liberals. The SDP may well break the mould of British politics, but it could do so in a way that is very different from that envisaged when it was launched with such high hopes on that memorable day in March 1981.

If the SDP does sink without trace in this fashion, its disappearance will be the cruellest trick yet played on Britain by its crazy electoral system. The failure of the SDP to emerge as a major political force could rob the country of the opportunity to come to terms, at long last, with its history of decline and failure in the twentieth century and to embark on a new course more suited to its position as a relatively poor but curiously resourceful post-industrial society, in some ways, perhaps, the first of its kind in the world.

'*We're off! Er . . . where are we going?*'
(Star, 26 March 1981)

Notes

CHAPTER 1: INTRODUCTION

1. Quoted in *The Times*, 11 April 1981.
2. Interview with the author in Plymouth, 9 May 1981.
3. Leading article in *The Times*, 10 February 1981.

CHAPTER 2: THE BRITISH POLITICAL TRADITION

1. *The Times*, 24 March 1981.
2. Quoted in K. O. Morgan, *Consensus and Disunity: The Lloyd George Coalition Government 1918–1922* (Oxford: Clarendon Press, 1979), p. 112.
3. *Economist,* 21 February 1948.
4. Jo Grimond, *Memoirs* (London: Heinemann, 1979), p. 216.
5. Peter Clarke, *Liberals and Social Democrats* (Cambridge: Cambridge University Press, 1978), p. 5.

CHAPTER 3: CHANGES IN THE 1970s

1. David Butler and Donald Stokes, *Political Change in Britain*, 2nd edn. (London: Macmillan, 1974).
2. Quoted in D. Butler and U. Kitzinger, *The 1975 Referendum* (London: Macmillan, 1976), p. 169.
3. ibid., p. 168.
4. A. Crosland, *Social Democracy in Europe*, Fabian Society pamphlet (London: Fabian Society, 1975), p. 10.
5. The polls were published in *The Times* on 30 September 1972 and 17 January 1980.

CHAPTER 4: THE TRANSFORMATION OF THE LABOUR PARTY

1. A. Crosland, *The Future of Socialism* (London: Jonathan Cape, 1956, 1964).
2. D. Taverne, *The Future of the Left* (London: Jonathan Cape, 1974), p. 21.
3. ibid., p. 22.

4. Collin Mellors, *The British MP* (Farnborough: Saxon House, 1978), p. 74.
5. George Orwell, *Collected Essays, Journalism and Letters* (London: Secker and Warburg, 1968), vol. 3, p. 5.
6. *Political Studies*, vol. 27, no. 1, (1979), p. 112.
7. Taverne, *The Future of the Left*, p. 50.
8. ibid., p. 84.
9. ibid., p. 86.
10. *The Times*, 16 June 1975.
11. *Socialist Commentary*, vol. 40 (1976), p. 9.
12. *Encounter*, July 1979, pp. 17–18.
13. S. Haseler, *The Tragedy of Labour* (Oxford: Basil Blackwell, 1980), pp. 73, 231–2.

CHAPTER 5: THE BIRTH OF THE SOCIAL DEMOCRATIC PARTY

1. Quoted in *The Times*, 22 May 1980.
2. Quoted in *The Times*, 25 July 1980.
3. Quoted in the *Listener*, 25 June 1981, p. 804.
4. Quoted in *The Times*, 29 November 1980.
5. Sections of Owen's memo were quoted in the *Guardian*, 25 March 1981, and in *The Times*, 26 March 1981.

CHAPTER 6: WHAT SORT OF PARTY IS THE SDP?

1. The story is told, *inter alia*, in the *Guardian*, 27 March 1981.
2. Published in London by Jonathan Cape in 1981.
3. Quoted in *The Times*, 25 March 1981.
4. Quoted in the *Guardian*, 24 February 1981.
5. *The Times*, 2 February 1981.
6. Quoted in *The Times*, 5 June 1981.
7. Quoted in *The Times*, 30 March 1981.
8. ibid.
9. Interview with the author at the launch of the Cornish provisional branch of the SDP, Redruth, 8 May 1981.
10. Interview with the author, 2 April 1981.
11. Quoted in *Time Out*, 10–16 April 1981.
12. R. Jenkins, *What Matters Now* (London: Fontana, 1972), p. 24.

CHAPTER 7: WHAT DOES THE SDP STAND FOR?

1. Quoted in *The Times*, 27 March 1981.
2. David Owen, *Face the Future* (London: Jonathan Cape, 1981).
3. Shirley Williams, *Politics is for People* (London: Penguin, 1981).
4. ibid., p. 16.

5. Owen, *Face the Future*, p. 6.
6. David Marquand, 'Taming Leviathan: Social Democracy and Decentralisation' (unpublished lecture, 1980), pp. 3–4.
7. Owen, *Face the Future*, p. 12.
8. ibid., p. 165.
9. ibid., p. 15.
10. M. Young, *Bigness is the Enemy of Humanity* (London: SDP, 1981).
11. Evan Luard, *Socialism Without the State* (London: Macmillan, 1979).
12. Marquand, 'Taming Leviathan', p. 8.
13. ibid., p. 26.
14. Young, *Bigness is the Enemy of Humanity*, p. 20.
15. Williams, *Politics is for People*, p. 23.
16. Owen, *Face the Future*, pp. 66–7.

CHAPTER 8: BREAKING THE MOULD?

1. Quoted in articles entitled 'The Centre in Turmoil' which appeared in *The Times,* 17 and 18 February 1981.
2. Reported in *The Times*, 7 May 1981.
3. Quoted in *The Times*, 16 February 1981.
4. I have been greatly helped in compiling these figures illustrating the performance of breakaway parties abroad by the Press Offices of the Dutch and Italian Embassies and by information contained in an article entitled 'Social democracy doesn't thrive abroad', which appeared in the *Economist*, 28 March–3 April 1981.
5. The Bristol analysis is described in an article by Peter Kellner and Gordon Reece in the *New Statesman*, 10 April 1981. I have taken my figures from that article.
6. I learned of this Liberal study from John Vincent's splendid article on the SDP, 'Looking for the Middle Way', in the *Times Literary Supplement*, 17 April 1981, pp. 423–4.
7. *Labour Weekly*, 1 May 1981.
8. Matthew Oakeshott, *The Road from Limehouse to Westminster: Prospects for a Radical Realignment at the General Election* (London: Radical Centre for Democratic Studies in Industry and Society, 1981).
9. I am indebted for the point about the decline in marginal seats to the fascinating study by Michael Steed and John Curtice, 'Electoral Choice and the Production of Government: The Changing Operation of the UK Electoral System since 1955', which was presented as a paper to the annual conference of the Political Studies Association in April 1981.

Further Reading

CHAPTER 2: THE BRITISH POLITICAL TRADITION

Bradley, Ian *The Optimists: Themes and Personalities in Victorian Liberalism* (London: Faber and Faber, 1980).

Bradley, Ian 'Attempts to Form a Centre Party in Britain, 1880–1980', *History Today,* vol. 31 (1981), pp. 41–3.

Butler, David, and Sloman, Anne *British Political Facts 1900–1979,* 5th edn. (London: Macmillan, 1980).

Clarke, Peter *Liberals and Social Democrats* (Cambridge: Cambridge University Press, 1978).

Grimond, Jo *Memoirs* (London: Heinemann, 1979).

Pelling, Henry *The Origins of the Labour Party*, 2nd edn. (Oxford: Clarendon Press, 1965).

Vincent, John *The Formation of the British Liberal Party* 1857–1868 Harmondsworth: Penguin, 1972).

CHAPTER 3: CHANGES IN THE 1970s

Butler, David, and Stokes, Donald *Political Change in Britain*, 2nd edn. (London: Macmillan, 1974).

Butler, David, and Kitzinger, Uwe *The 1975 Referendum* (London: Macmillan, 1976).

Crosland, Anthony *Social Democracy in Europe*, Fabian Society pamphlet (London: Fabian Society, 1975).

Henig, Stanley (ed.) *Political Parties in the European Community* (London: Allen and Unwin, 1979).

CHAPTER 4: THE TRANSFORMATION OF THE LABOUR PARTY

Crosland, Anthony *The Future of Socialism*, 2nd edn. (London: Jonathan Cape, 1964).

Haseler, Stephen *The Tragedy of Labour* (Oxford: Basil Blackwell, 1980).

Howell, David *British Social Democracy* (London: Croom Helm, 1980).

Marquand, David 'Inquest on a Movement', *Encounter,* July 1979, pp. 8–18.
Taverne, Dick *The Future of the Left: Lincoln and After* (London: Jonathan Cape, 1974).

CHAPTER 5: THE BIRTH OF THE SOCIAL DEMOCRATIC PARTY
CHAPTER 6: WHAT SORT OF PARTY IS THE SDP?

There are, as yet, no books about the SDP apart from this one. No doubt there soon will be.

CHAPTER 7: WHAT DOES THE SDP STAND FOR?

Luard, Evan *Socialism Without the State* (London: Macmillan, 1979).
Luard, Evan *Socialism at the Grassroots*, Fabian Society pamphlet (London: Fabian Society, 1980).
Marquand, David 'Taming Leviathan: Social Democracy and Decentralisation' (unpublished lecture, 1980).
Owen, David *Face the Future* (London: Jonathan Cape, 1981).
Williams, Shirley *Politics is for People* (London: Allen Lane/ Penguin, 1981).
Young, Michael *Bigness is the Enemy of Humanity* (London: SDP, 1981).

CHAPTER 8: BREAKING THE MOULD?

Oakeshott, Matthew *The Road from Limehouse to Westminster: Prospects for a Radical Realignment at the General Election* (London: Radical Centre for Democratic Studies in Industry and Society, 1981).
Steed, Michael, and Curtice, John 'Electoral Choice and the Production of Government: The Changing Operation of the UK Electoral System since 1955' (unpublished paper, University of Manchester, 1981).
Steed, Michael, and Faull, David *First Past the Post: The Great British Class Handicap* (London: Liberal Publications Dept., 1980).

Index

Details of our complete list are available in the following areas: Politics and Sociology, Social Policy, Education, Economics, Soviet Studies and Women's Studies. Copies of catalogues and further information on particular titles can be obtained from Promotion Services Department, Martin Robertson and Co. Ltd., P.O. Box 87, Oxford OX4 1LB.

SUBJECT WOMEN

ANN OAKLEY

The position of women in contemporary western culture is more complex than ever before. Ann Oakley's book is a powerful analysis of what it means to be female in society today.

'*An exciting, bracing and at times very inspiring book.*'
Marina Warner, THE SUNDAY TIMES

'*The book should make converts to feminism as well as providing information for women who are already feminists . . . it is admirable – clear, sane and reliable.*'
Janet Radcliffe Richards, THE GUARDIAN

Published May 1981

WHAT UNEMPLOYMENT MEANS
ADRIAN SINFIELD

Adrian Sinfield's unique and compelling book analyses what it means to be unemployed in Britain today.

'*Adrian Sinfield is concerned, and bitterly angry, about the wilful ignorance of those who are sufficiently well placed, geographically and otherwise, to avoid seeing the realities of unemployment . . . in a short and highly readable book . . . he sets out all the facts in which noses ought to be rubbed.*'
Mervyn Jones, THE GUARDIAN

'*. . . a wide-ranging and thought-provoking review of the impact of unemployment on those who must bear it and on the nature of the society which inflicts it.*'
Frances Williams, THE TIMES

Published February 1981

THE ULTIMATE RESOURCE
JULIAN SIMON

The real shortage is people.

So argues Julian Simon in this provocative and lively attack on those who sound alarms against population growth and resource use. He challenges conventional beliefs about the scarcity of energy and natural resources, the pollution of the environment, the effects of immigration and the validity of forecasts about population change.

'The book is thought provoking in the best sense of this hackneyed term. Altogether this is a very good book.'
Professor P. T. Bauer, LONDON SCHOOL OF ECONOMICS

September 1981

THE OTHER PRICE OF
BRITAIN'S OIL

W. G. CARSON

Britain is now reaping the benefit of the great oil and gas bonanza in the North Sea but at what price?

In this major new study W. G. Carson argues that the price paid in terms of death and injury to oil workers has been much too high. Has the regulation of safety and enforcement of existing legislation been downgraded in the rush to get the oil out quickly?

The author convincingly shows that the popular image of offshore danger is at odds with the reality of North Sea oil exploration. Drawing on detailed evidence from accident files and other sources he reveals that the vast majority of casualties in the North Sea result from relatively mundane and easily controllable factors; factors familiar to anyone concerned with the regulation of industrial safety in general.

The Other Price of Britain's Oil confronts the less creditable – and less publicised – side of the North Sea success story.

November 1981

THE POLITICS OF POVERTY
DAVID DONNISON

From 1975 to its dissolution in 1980, David Donnison acted as chairman of the Supplementary Benefits Commission, working on the administration and reform of one of the most important, and contentious, set of social measures for alleviating poverty in Britain.

This book tells the inside story of what was achieved and how, and gives a unique insight into the policymaking process in British government.

The Supplementary Benefits Commission is no more, but the problems of poverty and deprivation are more in evidence than ever. David Donnison uses his knowledge and experience to make an acute analysis of the experience of poverty in Britain today, and he puts forward a positive programme of measures to combat it and to try and create a more just and equal society.

November 1981